Applying Depth of Knowledge and Cognitive Rigor

APPLYING DEPTH OF KNOWLEDGE AND COGNITIVE RIGOR

An Educator's Guide to Supporting Deeper Learning

Karin Hess

Foreword by Barbara R. Blackburn

TEACHERS COLLEGE PRESS
TEACHERS COLLEGE | COLUMBIA UNIVERSITY
NEW YORK AND LONDON

Published by Teachers College Press,® 1234 Amsterdam Avenue, New York, NY 10027

Front cover icons: Lightbulb by Vimal, Cloud by Colleen Cameron, Puzzle by Untashable, Labyrinth by Doodle Icons, Hands by Juicy Fish, and Flowchart by Yoyon Pujiyono, all from the Noun Project.

Interior Icons: Clipboard by SISWANTORO, Compass by RULI, Discussion icon by Vincenze Studio, Pencil by pramana, Thought Bubble by murmur, Video icon by Diding jamaludin, all from the Noun Project (https://www.thenounproject.com).

Library of Congress Cataloging-in-Publication Data is available at loc.gov

ISBN 978-0-8077-8676-5 (paper)
ISBN 978-0-8077-8677-2 (hardcover)
ISBN 978-0-8077-8291-0 (ebook)

Printed on acid-free paper
Manufactured in the United States of America

Contents

Foreword

Rigor, particularly in education, has been discussed, debated, and misunderstood for the last 30 years. What began as a policy discussion (how to put more students in honors classes) led to misinterpretations and even resistance about the word itself (rigor vs. rigor mortis). The teachers and leaders I worked with became increasingly frustrated. As one teacher shared with me, "I'm tired of being told to incorporate rigor without being shown how to do it."

Although Bloom's taxonomy (created in 1956 and revised in 2001) and, more recently, Webb's Depth of Knowledge (first published in 1997) helped to add clarity about rigor, educators were still frustrated. Is Bloom's better than Webb's? Are they both about verbs? Just tell me, what does rigor look like?

I have (hopefully) helped with that discussion through my books and workshops, but teachers continued to need a more structured framework—something that would take them from planning to assessment and everything in between.

In the midst of my journey to better explain to educators what rigor looks like at all stages of teaching, I was excited to discover Karin's Cognitive Rigor Matrices (CRMs). She had taken Bloom's taxonomy and integrated it with Webb's Depth of Knowledge framework, providing practical examples at all levels of rigor—first for core subject areas (Reading and Listening, Math and Science, Written and Oral Communication, and Social Studies and Humanities) and then for special subject areas (Fine Arts, Health and Physical Education, World Languages, and Career and Technical Education). How smart! She took what teachers were already familiar with and made it even more practical.

As I shared the Hess CRMs with teachers, they continued to want more. What are they? How do I use them to plan? How do they factor into instruction and assessment? In other words, give me a guide on *how* to use them. Leaders also reminded me that it would be critical to know the research base for the matrices. All of us have seen—and been dismayed by—the latest and greatest fad that wasn't research-based. That's why I was so pleased when Karin told me she was writing this book, a how-to playbook of sorts to help teachers apply the concepts of the Hess Cognitive Rigor Matrices in their classrooms that also incorporates the research for all aspects of her model. As I read the manuscript, I wasn't at all surprised to find it full of practical guidance, but I particularly appreciated the interactive applications readers can use for reflection. Although I am hesitant to prioritize any particular content, if you want an immediate "I can use this tomorrow" idea, jump right into Module 5, Applying a Cognitive Rigor Mindset to Deep Instruction. I found myself wishing I was back in the classroom so I could try the strategies.

The reality is that you could start with any module, whether it is planning, instruction, assessment, or working with standards. Each module is unique and has the capability to transform your classroom. I encourage you to consider this a journey to higher levels of rigor. This book is a master class on applying cognitive rigor, and Karin is an excellent guide.

—Barbara R. Blackburn

Module Activities and Additional Resources

MODULE 1

- **Activity 1.1:** Analyze one level of Bloom
- **Activity 1.2**: Bloom vs. Webb: Explain your thinking in an elevator pitch
- **Activity 1.3:** Analyzing the intended Depth of Knowledge (DOK) levels of learning or assessment tasks
- **Activity 1.4:** Time to reflect—Has your understanding of DOK changed or been refined in some way?
- View the grade 3 video, "Tiny House Project," at https://www.pblworks.org/video-tiny-house-project
- **Activity 1.5:** Time to apply—Create one sample task for each DOK level

MODULE 2

- **Activity 2.1:** Pre-Post Self-Assessment: What is your current understanding of DOK?
- Watch Part 3 of Karin's Master Class on applying cognitive rigor, "Are Your Students Thinking Deeply, or Just Working Harder?" describing scaffolding strategies at https://youtu.be/WYSYWe2OvcM (8:44 minutes).
- **Activity 2.2:** Examine a sample learning progression
- **Activity 2.3:** Practice activity—*It's what comes after the verb!*
- **Activity 2.4:** Time to reflect—Post Self-Assessment
- Watch a review of common misconceptions in the webinar, "Looking for Rigor in All the Right Places," at https://www.youtube.com/watch?v=gXFb5gdcogw (from minute 4:30 to 25:10)

MODULE 3

- **Activity 3.1:** Examining six deeper learning competencies
- **Activity 3.2:** What does deep instruction include?
- Watch a short video of John Hattie explaining his research at https://www.visiblelearning.com
- **Activity 3.3:** Watch (and reflect on) a TEDx Talk with Marc Chun, "Diving into Deeper Learning," at https://www.youtube.com/watch?v=k6BmbdzPcrY.
- Watch a webinar about the SOLO taxonomy, "5 Ways to Power-up Your Teaching," at https://www.youtube.com/watch?v=nStNc0ZCkH4.
- **Activity 3.4:** Time to reflect—When have you acquired skills and knowledge that you later transferred to complete a more complex, real-world task?

MODULE 4

- Watch a short video showing how an elementary teacher adds clarity to success criteria by setting parameters at https://www.youtube.com//watch?v=8S3MuIdH14s.
- **Activity 4.1:** Time to apply—Unwrap a content standard and develop performance expectations

Activity 4.2: Time to apply—Developing success criteria at different DOK levels

MODULE 5

Activity 5.1: What does cognitive rigor look and sound like?

Watch part 1 of Karin's Master Class on applying cognitive rigor, "Are Your Students Thinking Deeply?" Dr. Hess summarizes some of the related research, "6 Indicators of Cognitive Rigor," at https://youtu.be/LMDF26tAjuc (18 minutes).

Download a full-color copy of "6 Indicators of Cognitive Rigor" at https://www.karin-hess.com/_files/ugd/5e86bd_f8e477542dc44d6e8ea6e57d2a6d4e10.pdf

Activity 5.2: Reflect on Hattie's 2023 research (instructional examples)

For more information and a video on sketchnoting, visit https://sketchyideas.co/what-are-sketchnotes-and-why-should-you-use-them/.

Watch a Kahn Academy video at https://www.youtube.com/watch?v=CZ5ne_mX5_I, and try sketching your notes.

Activity 5.3: Time to apply—Create a "Say It Another Way" template for a unit of study

Activity 5.4: Review strategies for making and supporting connections

Building Schema: Watch a short video, "Text Complexity Toolkit," summarizing some of the research about genre-specific schemas (text structures, discourse styles, etc.) at https://www.youtube.com/watch?v=N7we0ZcC6ig&t=288s.

Activity 5.5: Review strategies for building schemas

Activity 5.6: Observing teacher–student interactions using the Lesson Observation Form (Appendix D, p. 111)

Watch "Boosting Engagement With Notices and Wonders" at https://www.youtube.com/watch?v=yp0QORzzvSs.

Activity 5.7: Apply TQE to a topic you teach

To better understand the Depth and Complexity Framework, you can find articles and videos at https://www.byrdseed.com/category/depth-and-complexity-icons.

Activity 5.8: Review strategies for generating questions

Watch a video of a kindergarten teacher guiding her students to transfer their learning to plan to teach a lesson to preschool students. Access the video at https://eleducation.org/resources/going-deep-with-kindergartners-with-problem-based-tasks-in-math/.

Activity 5.9: Review strategies for defining a challenge

Watch a video of 10th-graders engaging in a Socratic Circle and how the teacher keeps them on track at https://vimeo.com/54871334.

Watch a video of middle school students engaging in collaborative discussions using the support of "talk move" reminders at https://www.edutopia.org/video/encouraging-academic-conversations-talk-moves.

Activity 5.10: Review strategies for tackling complex tasks with collaboration

Activity 5.11: Analyze a unit of study—Where are the . . . Drills? Scrimmages? Games?

Watch part 2 of Karin's Master Class on applying cognitive rigor, "Are Your Students Thinking Deeply?" Dr. Hess describes how she merged two complexity models: Bloom and Webb's DOK to create the Hess Cognitive Rigor Matix and discusses the mental processing needed to create as well as answer questions of increasing complexity. You can access the video at https://youtu.be/NeOtmJr8Q3k (17:47 minutes).

MODULE 6

Activity 6.1: What is high-quality performance-based assessment?

Activity 6.2: What makes learning meaningful to students?

Activity 6.3: Using Tool 9 to analyze a performance-based assessment (PBA; see Figure 6.1 and Appendix C, pp. 102–104)

Watch part 4 of Karin's Master Class on applying cognitive rigor, "Are Your Students Thinking Deeply, or Just Working Harder?"

Dr. Hess describes balancing DOK levels in summative assessments. Access the video at https://youtu.be/cGTBDFRo200 (11:17 minutes).

Watch a short video, "Karin Hess's 'Handy' Brain Model," explaining connections among cognitive science, engagement, and student involvement designing PBAs. Access the video at https://www.youtube.com/watch?v=DrGggsJWgQk (8 minutes).

Activity 6.4: Analyze sample PBA prompts and then create your own prompt

To better understand the purposes of formative assessment, view a video clip, "What is formative assessment?," at http://artsassessmentforlearning.org/about-assessment/.

Watch the video, "What can we learn from analyzing student work?," illustrating the student work analysis process in action, using Tool 12.

[Part 1] Dr. Hess provides an overview of the importance of her D-I-E approach to analyzing student work at https://www.youtube.com/watch?v=lwXcm1rbtFk (8 minutes).

[Part 2] Dr. Hess walks teachers through how to complete the student work analysis (note that in the video, this is numbered Tool 11) at https://youtu.be/w3l47rq6nBI (9 minutes).

[Part 3] Dr. Hess guides teachers in analyzing student work from a kindergarten math problem solving PBA at https://youtu.be/7JttirFB5ak (19 minutes).

[Part 4] Dr. Hess guides teachers in analyzing student work from a grade 3 writing PBA at https://youtu.be/wjuDs5N7LDs (16 minutes).

Activity 6.5: Choose either Tool 10 or Tool 13 and use it to analyze a formative assessment strategy you currently use or the flow of lessons in one of your units of study

Acknowledgments

I would like to express gratitude for the people and ideas that have shaped my thinking and learning over the years about depth of knowledge and cognitive rigor. My understanding has been deepened by three major influences: people who have developed thinking and complexity models; people who have researched and written about cognitive science and learning transfer; and people who have worked with me, questioned me about my ideas, and shared their own invaluable insights with me. This book honors all of those people.

Throughout my career, I've explored a variety of thinking and complexity models. But if I hadn't randomly come across a 1997 paper by Norman Webb, this book—and much of my work—might have evolved differently. It was Webb's description of a depth of knowledge framework used in alignment studies that began my own deep dive into how to design high-quality assessments and, more importantly, how educators could create the classroom conditions so all students would learn to their fullest potential. To say the least, my work with assessment, cognitive rigor, and learning progressions has been greatly influenced by Webb's seminal work, as well as by analyzing and sometimes integrating DOK thinking with other models (e.g., Bloom, 1956; Porter & Smithson, 2001).

While exploring applications of depth of knowledge, I was also taking a deep dive into cognitive science and what it means for a student to transfer learning in new contexts. The books that have most impacted my thinking were *How People Learn: Brain, Mind, Experience, and School* (National Research Council, 1999), *Knowing What Students Know* (National Academies Press, 2001), and *Understanding by Design* (Wiggins & McTighe, 2005). I was also continually making connections with John Hattie's research syntheses (2009, 2023) and the teacher and student strategies that best support deep engagement and learning transfer. Operationalizing a student's ability to transfer learning has become one of my big epiphanies about depth of knowledge and cognitive rigor. It's a simple connection: A shift in DOK levels leads to a shift in teacher–student roles during learning. A shift in teacher–student roles moves students from taking in and reproducing information to constructing knowledge and broadening meaning.

Theories are great, but practical applications are even better! I've worked with thousands of educators across the globe—from Australia to American schools in South Korea and Nicaragua, and throughout all of the United States and U.S. territories. I am most grateful for the contributions and feedback from practitioners who have worked with depth of knowledge and my cognitive rigor matrices over the years. When teachers asked me, "Aren't Bloom's taxonomy and Webb's framework the same?," I answered the question by developing my first rigor matrix. When teachers asked me, "What does this look like in fine arts or world languages?" I worked with them to test out new content-specific applications of DOK. When instructional coaches and school leaders asked me, "How can we use your matrix to observe teaching practices?," I worked to develop and field-test my "Looking for Rigor" walk-through tool (Hess, 2023) based on observable DOK level indicators. Educator questions have always pushed my thinking.

For this book, several educators graciously agreed to be interviewed by me. I've included some of their ideas and a few brief scenarios throughout the book to illustrate the many ways depth of knowledge and cognitive rigor can be implemented in schools, with fidelity. I extend my heartfelt appreciation to these thought partners for helping me and other educators stretch and deepen our understanding of applying cognitive rigor.

- Nathan Auck, STEM Coordinator, Personalized Competency-Based Learning (PCBL) Specialist, Utah State Board of Education
- Karen Boch, Gallia-Vinton ESC Administrative Associate, Rio Grande, OH
- Kristina Fulton, curriculum and instruction specialist, PA
- Tom Mungovan, Graphic Design and Creative Media Instructor, Concord Regional Technical Center, Concord, NH
- Norm Potter, Author, Owner of Structured Creativity Consulting, OH (www.structuredcreativityconsulting.com)
- Char Shryock, Education Leadership Consulting LLC, OH (https://bit.ly/charshryock)
- Laurie Gagnon, Former Quality Performance Assessment Director at the Center for Collaborative Education, currently CompetencyWorks Director, Aurora Institute (https://aurora-institute.org)
- Steve Rothenberg, former Director Concord Regional Technical Center and CTE consultant, Concord, NH (steve@rothenbergcg.com)
- Kirsten Soroko, MEd, CAGS, Director of Personalized Learning and Growth, Pinkerton Academy, NH
- Adam Watson, Digital Learning Consultant, Ohio Valley Educational Cooperative, KY

Last, but certainly not least, I'd like to thank my graphic artist, Meena Mehta of 2M Graphics, who for many years has assisted me in the design and beautiful look of my CRM tools and posters, and to Allison Scott and the staff at Teachers College Press for their support in making this book beautiful and useful to educators.

Applying Depth of Knowledge and Cognitive Rigor

Introduction

How often have you come across the terms depth of knowledge (DOK) or rigor in curricular and assessment resources? I see them everywhere! Yet, over the years, I've found that there is a lack of consistency across sources in how DOK and rigor are defined, how DOK levels are interpreted and applied, and for what purpose. In many cases, these descriptions do not reflect what the research defines as "deep learning" or learning transfer. This book describes my evolving thinking about these ideas.

In the early 2000s, drawing from the work of Norman Webb (2002, 2005), I first used DOK level descriptors to design alignment studies for my work in several states. In an alignment study, reviewers analyze state tests in order to "match" each test question with the content standard assessed and the *intended* DOK level for that question (conceptual understanding = DOK 2, performing procedural skills = DOK 1, supporting claims with evidence = DOK 3, etc.). Protocols regarding the range of DOK levels of test questions are aligned with the state's overall test blueprint to ensure that each year's test consistently "balances" the specific content assessed and the overall intended complexity. In other words, a test blueprint identifies what content (standards) will be assessed at every grade level and determines how challenging the overall test will be. For example, 30% of test questions will be at DOK 1, 40% will be at DOK 2, and so on.

Eventually my work with DOK led to guiding educators across the United States in curriculum and assessment development work, applying my expanding understanding of DOK to develop standards or "unpack" existing standards to determine both the content knowledge to be learned and to describe how students would demonstrate that learning (Hess, 2018; Hess, in Hougen & Smartt, 2020). The result of this work was often used to design everything from state grade-level tests to local units of study and performance-based assessments.

Today, it's quite common to find collaborative teams (professional learning communities [PLCs], grade-level teams, etc.) applying what I call "a cognitive rigor mindset" to develop rigorous learning and assessment tasks. And, as with all applications of a great idea, the results of these efforts have ranged from a surface-level grasp and application of DOK to a deeper and more meaningful understanding.

So, because I've spent more than 2 decades writing about and working with depth of knowledge and expanding applications of cognitive rigor across content areas, it may seem a bit strange for me to be returning to the basics of what DOK is, what it is not, and how to apply a cognitive rigor mindset with fidelity so that every student's learning goal is to achieve deep understanding. That is exactly what this book is intended to guide educators to do.

Through interactive discussions, reflections, and practice activities, educators will be guided to

- develop a shared understanding of depth of knowledge and its relationship to cognitive rigor and engagement;
- use descriptors in the Hess Cognitive Rigor Matrices to analyze DOK levels in curricular materials across content areas and grade levels;
- explore the relationships among DOK, standards, and planning for deep instruction;
- identify strategies that help students move from conceptual understanding to the ability to deepen and transfer their learning to new or unfamiliar situations; and
- apply a cognitive rigor mindset to create actionable standards-based or competency-based assessments that uncover deeper thinking.

Table 0.1. Six Big Ideas When Applying DOK and Cognitive Rigor

1. There have always been a variety of thinking and complexity models available to educators. However, not all models are equally effective for planning and assessing deep learning and learning transfer. To be successful in systemically deepening student learning, educators must develop a shared understanding of what cognitive rigor is and how to apply it in support of deep learning for every student.	Your Thoughts? Questions?
2. Applications of DOK and cognitive rigor are widespread; still, misconceptions abound in how these concepts are being applied. Dispelling myths and correcting misinterpretations are part of building a shared understanding.	Your Thoughts? Questions?
3. We've learned from cognitive science that every content domain has a unique schema. Mental schemas are the way our brains organize and process information. DOK applications should reflect domain-specific schemas; planning for deep instruction and learning transfer should reflect how the brain learns.	Your Thoughts? Questions?
4. Shifting from DOK 1–2 to DOK 3–4 changes the roles of teachers and students during instruction—leading to opportunities for students to engage more deeply and transfer what they've learned. Performance-based assessments are the best way to assess (near vs. far) transfer of learning in new contexts.	Your Thoughts? Questions?
5. Standards are more than just nouns and verbs. Standards (and competencies) describe *what* content will be learned. Performance expectations describe *how* students will engage and demonstrate evidence of that learning. Performance expectations are often more useful to educators than the actual verb(s) included in content standards when planning curriculum, instruction, and assessments.	Your Thoughts? Questions?
6. Applying a "cognitive rigor mindset" to designing formative and summative assessments can lead to deeper learning for every student, but only when we consider each student's learning needs and how to strategically use scaffolding for different (and specific) purposes.	Your Thoughts? Questions?

The basics of defining DOK will only be the starting point as you work through the modules of this book. Consider this a "master class" in applying cognitive rigor, as you ponder my six big ideas—epiphanies that have come to me as I've worked with various applications of DOK and cognitive rigor for different purposes. On your own or with others, take a moment to read each of my big ideas (Table 0.1) and add your own related thoughts, questions, reflections, or sketchnotes. Does the big idea resonate with you? Does it challenge your current thinking or cause some cognitive dissonance? Does it validate what you currently believe and do now?

HOW TO USE THIS BOOK

Think of yourself as a coach and this book as your playbook. A coach's playbook offers options for strategies to use in different situations. In order for players to be prepared for a variety of situations, coaches need to teach skills and strategies and allow opportunities for practice and feedback so that eventually each player can use them independently and metacognitively. A coach needs to decide, "Is my goal to plan practice drills for learning concepts and skills in isolation; to provide opportunities to integrate skills and concepts in a scrimmage-like activity; or to guide players to independently make strategic decisions and apply skills and concepts while playing a game?"

All of these purposes for learning are important: acquiring a foundation, building conceptual understanding, and deepening or extending thinking. While there is no particular order for exploring the concepts, tools, and strategies in each module, there will be particular situations when one topic is more useful to you than another. If your purpose is to build a common language around DOK and cognitive rigor, start with Modules 1 and 2. If you and your colleagues have already built a solid understanding of DOK and cognitive rigor, choose a module that best meets your current needs—exploring deep learning and learning transfer, analyzing standards or competencies, planning learning activities or assessment tasks, or coaching and providing feedback to teachers.

When applying depth of knowledge and cognitive rigor for different purposes, your role as an educator will be cyclical—from directing learning to strategic coaching that expands on learning, and back again to directing or coaching to add new layers of understanding. This is true regardless of whether the learners are you and your colleagues or you and your students. You get to decide what learning is most appropriate for you right now.

HOW THE BOOK IS ORGANIZED

Each stand-alone module is framed by frequently asked questions and supporting research. Modules are designed to be interactive, moving readers through an exploration of ideas, short videos with examples, opportunities to practice and apply, and questions prompting readers to transfer ideas to their own practice. Modules have several possible uses: to guide professional learning for new teachers or educators new to DOK, as a refresher course in DOK, or to extend thinking about applications of DOK, cognitive rigor, and strategies that support deep learning. Modules can be used to guide individual learning but will be most impactful in a school setting when peers collaboratively investigate these concepts.

Module 1 lays the foundation for developing a shared understanding of depth of knowledge and its relationship to cognitive rigor. The module provides brief descriptions of several thinking and complexity models and explains how depth of knowledge and Bloom's taxonomy were merged to create the first Hess Cognitive Rigor Matrices (CRMs) and why other approaches were used when developing CRMs for fine arts, health and physical education, world languages, and career and technical education. This module addresses Big Ideas 1 and 3—developing a shared understanding of what cognitive rigor is and how to apply it in support of deep learning for every student and applying cognitive science to better understand how we learn. Key questions explored in Module 1 include the following:

- What is depth of knowledge, and how is it different from other thinking and complexity models, such as Bloom's taxonomy?
- What is the connection between cognitive rigor and DOK?
- How can we develop consistent language when we apply our understanding of DOK and cognitive rigor?
- What *could* learning look like at each of the four DOK levels?

Module 2 adds another layer to developing a shared understanding by debunking seven of the most common myths and misconceptions about DOK and rigor. The module begins with a pre-post anticipation guide. Readers can self-assess their current understanding and revisit and refine their responses after reading, viewing, or discussing ideas presented in Module 2. This module addresses Big Idea 2—the need to dispel myths and correct misinterpretations in order to build a shared understanding about how and when to apply DOK and cognitive rigor. Key questions explored in Module 2 include the following:

- Can *all* students—meaning all ages, all grade levels, all ability levels—actually engage in complex work?
- Are there specific verbs or question prompts always associated with each DOK level?
- Is DOK intended to be used as a taxonomy or perhaps as a learning progression?

Module 3 continues the theme of developing a shared understanding of cognitive rigor—introducing the Hewlett Foundation's (2013) Six Broad Competencies for Deep Learning and explaining how they generally connect with DOK levels and learning transfer. To better understand what it means to transfer learning, a brief timeline of researcher and educator perspectives is summarized to reveal important implications for operationalizing deep instruction, since deep instruction leads to deeper student engagement, a requisite of learning transfer. A brief comparison of DOK levels and the SOLO taxonomy levels (Biggs & Collis, 1982) is also included to clarify thinking about what near-far transfer could look like. This module addresses Big Ideas 3 and 4—applying cognitive science to better understand how learning develops and how shifting teacher–student roles during instruction leads to deeper engagement and learning transfer. Key questions explored in Module 3 include the following:

- How are deep learning, learning transfer, and DOK connected?
- What is deep instruction, and how can I use a cognitive rigor mindset to teach for transfer?
- Why, how, and when does a teacher's approach—or role—need to shift at each DOK level if deep learning is the goal?

Module 4 illustrates how to apply an understanding of cognitive rigor to "unwrap" content (standards and competencies) in order to determine the many ways students might demonstrate learning. Practice activities include examining the potential DOK levels implied by how standards are written and generating performance expectations and success criteria that increase in complexity. This module addresses Big Idea 5—developing an understanding of how content (standards/competencies) and DOK are related helps to establish performance expectations when planning curriculum and instruction and developing assessments. Key questions explored in Module 4 include the following:

- How do we use the Hess CRMs to accurately interpret our standards or competencies with regard to task complexity or performance expectations?
- How are cognitive rigor, standards/competencies, and success criteria related?
- How can curriculum design articulate the path to deeper learning for students and the transfer goals they are working toward?

Module 5 defines six observable indicators of cognitive rigor with instructional examples that support deep instruction. This module addresses Big Ideas 3 and 4—applying cognitive science to better understand how learning develops and how shifting teacher–student roles during instruction leads to deeper engagement and learning transfer. Key questions explored in Module 5 include the following:

- How can DOK and cognitive rigor be applied when planning learning activities?
- When a standard is based on a basic skill that only requires surface-level understanding, how can we deepen the DOK engagement?
- Is there a way to apply DOK with daily planning and not have it be too cumbersome?

Module 6 introduces a set of classroom-tested assessment planning tools (found in Appendix C) for analyzing formative, summative, and performance-based assessments and interpreting student assessment evidence to make "next steps" instructional decisions. This module addresses Big Idea 6, that designing formative and summative assessments can lead to deeper learning for every student, but only when we consider each student's learning needs and how to strategically use scaffolding for different (and specific) purposes. Key questions explored in Module 6 include the following:

- What are the "need-to-knows" for developing high-quality formative, summative, or performance-based assessments?
- DOK 3 and DOK 4 assessments take so long. Are they worth the time?
- How can transfer goals be used to design a performance-based assessment?
- Does every student need to take the same assessment? If different assessments are used to assess the same skills and concepts, can I use the same scoring rubric?

Developing a Shared Understanding of DOK and Cognitive Rigor

Key Questions Explored in Module 1:

- What is depth of knowledge, and how is it different from other thinking and complexity models, such as Bloom's taxonomy?
- What is the connection between cognitive rigor and DOK?
- How can we develop consistent language when we apply our understanding of DOK and cognitive rigor?
- What *could* learning look like at each of the four DOK levels?

Over the past decades, a variety of thinking models have caused educators to consider better ways to plan lessons or guide students in developing critical and creative thinking skills. Howard Gardner's multiple intelligences theory (2006) broadened the definition of intelligence, outlining eight different types of intelligences: linguistic, logical/mathematical, spatial, bodily-kinesthetic, musical, interpersonal, intrapersonal, and naturalist. Gardner's theory states that everyone has all eight intelligences at varying degrees of proficiency; however, an individual's learning style is *unrelated* to the areas in which they are the most intelligent. For example, someone with linguistic intelligence may not necessarily learn best through writing and reading. As a teacher, multiple intelligences theory was intriguing to me, yet too abstract for me to know how to apply it in my daily lessons.

Conversely, using Edward de Bono's business management strategy of Six Thinking Hats (1999) was an easy way to get my students to see a problem from different perspectives. His structured approach—related to six different-colored hats—is used to enhance decision-making and group problem-solving. The blue hat focuses on managing the thinking process and overall problem context; the white hat represents seeking clarity using objective data and information; the red hat focuses on expressing emotions and using intuition and "gut" feelings; the black hat represents skepticism, identifying potential risks; the person with the yellow hat encourages positive thinking; and the green hat unleashes creativity. I used de Bono's model to get my students thinking divergently but found that it was not as effective if I wanted them to take a problem from idea generation to planning to full completion.

These were just two of the many "thinking" models I experimented with during my teaching years, while taking courses in gifted education. I always seemed to come back to Bloom's taxonomy (Bloom, 1956). The taxonomy was concrete enough that I could select verbs from different levels to design my lessons, and the hierarchy of the taxonomy made me think I could use it to plan and measure learning progress. Could it really be this simple? Ease of use might be one reason that Bloom's taxonomy is so familiar to most educators today.

I didn't realize I was searching for a more effective model that could describe deep learning until I came across Webb's Depth of Knowledge framework (Webb, 1997, 2002). This module explores how my thinking has evolved as I applied and compared the DOK framework to other models, eventually merging ideas to describe DOK and cognitive rigor in different content areas.

In 2005, I was asked a thoughtful question by members of a state-level committee working with me on the design of their state's new grade-level assessments. Like many other states, this state and their testing contractor had been using Bloom's taxonomy (1956) to describe test item difficulty. "But isn't Webb's DOK model just another way to describe the same thing as what Bloom's six levels do?" teachers asked me when I introduced the DOK framework and suggested a shift to using DOK-level descriptors instead of Bloom's taxonomy for determining the complexity of test items and the standards they aligned with.

I struggled at the time to clearly articulate the key differences between these two models, even though I knew they were not specifically addressing the same characteristics of complexity. On the plane home, I began to examine each model in greater depth and experimented with where the two models might overlap. Although related through their natural ties to the complexity of thought, I could see that Bloom's thinking levels and Webb's depth of knowledge levels differed in scope, application, and probably intent. To show where there were connections, I began to create a matrix that superimposed Bloom's taxonomy with Webb's Depth of Knowledge levels. Let's take a closer look at these two models to see the similarities and differences.

REEXAMINING BLOOM'S TAXONOMY

In 1956, Benjamin Bloom headed a group of educational psychologists who developed classification levels of intellectual behavior important in three areas of learning: affective growth (in *attitude*—feelings or emotions), cognitive growth (in *knowledge*—mental/intellectual skills), and psychomotor growth (manual or physical skills). Within the cognitive domain, Bloom identified six levels, ordering them from the simple recall/memorization of facts, as the lowest level, through increasingly more complex and abstract mental levels, to evaluation, considered to be the highest order. This taxonomy was used to categorize the levels of abstraction (types of thinking demanded) of questions that commonly occur in educational settings. Using the taxonomy levels for analysis, Bloom found that over 95% of the test questions students encounter at the college level require them to think only at the lowest possible level in the taxonomy—the recall of information.

The cognitive taxonomy, now commonly referred to as "Bloom's taxonomy," includes verbs associated with each level, starting with knowledge (*the simplest tasks*) and moving up the levels to comprehension, application, analysis, synthesis, and evaluation (*the most challenging tasks*). (See Table 1.1.) It is important to note that different sources list somewhat different verb examples to represent intellectual activity on each of Bloom's levels, and *sometimes the same verbs appear in more than one cognitive level.* (See Table 1.1: **EXPLAIN**, **WRITE**, **APPRAISE.**)

In 2001, the original taxonomy was updated by Lorin Anderson, a former student of Bloom, and David Krathwohl, one of Bloom's partners in devising the original taxonomy. The biggest change to the revised taxonomy was switching the order of levels, moving Synthesis-Create to the *highest* level of the taxonomy (Armstrong, 2017). Renamed Bloom's Cognitive Process Dimensions (and commonly referred to as "Revised Bloom"), terms describing each level were changed from nouns to verbs (e.g., knowledge became remember; comprehension became understand); however, the interpretation of the levels did not change—a learner was expected to master a lower level before moving on to the next higher level in the taxonomy. Some verbs in Revised Bloom stayed at the same level, some were moved to a different level (see underlining in Table 1.1: illustrate, categorize, predict), and other verbs disappeared completely (e.g., calculate, write). This illustrates one way that verbs alone do not differentiate DOK levels.

Educators, like me, initially found verbs in the taxonomies useful in lesson planning; but focusing only on verbs to determine increasing levels of cognitive demand, especially when verbs appeared in multiple levels, was, at best, inadequate. This was made even clearer when I began to analyze levels of Bloom using descriptions of the four DOK levels. One example I noticed was at the Apply level; carrying out a procedure for a given situation would probably be at a lower DOK level, whereas applying a procedure to an unfamiliar task, such as a problem-solving situation, would likely be listed at a higher DOK level.

I could also think of examples using verbs within the same level of the taxonomy that describe both less challenging and more challenging tasks. Consider these two examples at the Analyze level—break a

Table 1.1. Comparing Bloom's Taxonomy with Bloom's Cognitive Process Dimensions

Bloom's Taxonomy (1956)	Bloom's Cognitive Process Dimensions (2001)
Knowledge—Define, duplicate, label, list, name, memorize, order, recognize, relate, recall, state	**Remember**—Retrieve knowledge from long-term memory, recognize, recall, locate, identify
Comprehension—Classify, describe, discuss, **EXPLAIN**, express, identify, indicate, locate, recognize, report, review, select, translate	**Understand**—Construct meaning, clarify, paraphrase, represent, translate, illustrate, give examples, classify, categorize, summarize, infer a logical conclusion, generalize, predict, explain
Application—Apply, choose, demonstrate, dramatize, employ, illustrate, interpret, practice, use, sketch, **WRITE**	**Apply**—Carry out or use a procedure in a given situation; carry out or use/apply to an unfamiliar task
Analysis—Analyze, **APPRAISE**, **EXPLAIN**, calculate, categorize, compare, criticize, discriminate, examine, experiment	**Analyze**—Break into constituent parts, determine how parts relate, differentiate between relevant and irrelevant, organize, outline
Synthesis—Rearrange, assemble, collect, compose, create, design, develop, formulate, manage, plan, organize, **WRITE**	**Evaluate**—Make judgments based on criteria, check, detect inconsistencies/fallacies, critique, judge
Evaluation—**APPRAISE**, argue, assess, choose, compare, defend, estimate, **EXPLAIN**, judge, predict, rate, core, select, support, value, evaluate	**Create**—Put elements together to form a coherent whole, reorganize elements into new patterns/structures, generate, hypothesize, plan

Source: Adapted from Bloom's taxonomy (1956) and Bloom's Cognitive Process Dimensions (Anderson, et al., 2001).

sentence apart to see how parts relate versus break an essay apart to see how the parts relate. Adding content to the verb changes the complexity and how students must engage with the content by drawing on prior knowledge to successfully complete a task.

Activity 1.1: Analyze one level of Bloom

Can you come up with examples using descriptions or verbs in the same level of the Revised Bloom's taxonomy that describe tasks of varying complexity? How does applying different content change the overall complexity?

WEBB'S DEPTH OF KNOWLEDGE LEVELS FOR FOUR CONTENT AREAS

How each level is described—whether in a taxonomy or in other complexity models—is essential to categorizing task examples and understanding which types of tasks are expected to be more or less complex for students. Let's examine the clarity of the DOK Framework in distinguishing among the four levels.

In the late 1990s, Norman Webb developed his Depth of Knowledge (DOK) Framework for use in categorizing expectations and assessment tasks according to the complexity of engagement required for success (Webb et al., 2023). DOK levels could be used to determine how deeply students would need to *engage with the content* in order to successfully complete a task. Webb's DOK levels in four content areas—language arts (reading and writing), mathematics, science, and social studies—provided a common language for interpreting academic standards and the tasks used to assess standards (e.g., in formal alignment studies of state tests) and for local curriculum planning.

Table 1.2 provides Webb's general descriptions for determining alignment between test items and academic standards. Webb has noted that "many on-demand assessment instruments (standardized tests) will not include assessment activities that could be classified as level 4. However, standards, goals, and objectives can be stated so as to expect students to perform thinking at this level" (Webb, 2002, p. 8).

DOK levels are framed by *what students must do to engage with content* to be successful answering a question or completing a task: DOK 1 (memorize, recall, and reproduce), DOK 2 (use basic skills and concepts), DOK 3 (think strategically and use reasoning), and DOK 4 (use complex reasoning and investigation).

Table 1.2. DOK Level Descriptions of Test Items for Alignment Studies

DOK 1 Recall and Reproduction
Items require only a shallow understanding, such as using a dictionary to look up word meaning, using punctuation marks, or performing simple skills and procedures.
DOK 2 Skills and Concepts
Items require some mental processing, such as using context to determine word meaning, making predictions, summarizing key ideas, and making some decisions as to how to approach a routine problem or how to display data.
DOK 3 Strategic Thinking and Reasoning
Items or task prompts require students to use reasoning and planning to interpret abstract themes, to construct multi-paragraph essays, or to support claims, solutions, or conclusions with details, examples, and evidence.
DOK 4 Extended Thinking and Reasoning
Items or task prompts require students to use complex reasoning, planning, and investigation to design and conduct a project, analyze or synthesize information across multiple sources, or evaluate alternative solutions and perspectives. Assessment items at level 4 will probably be extended tasks with extended time provided; however, extended time is not a distinguishing factor of level 4 if the work is only repetitive and does not require significant conceptual understanding.

Source: Adapted from Webb (2002).

DOK levels describe increasingly complex tasks, often requiring the use of "many verbs," not just one!

Activity 1.2: Bloom vs. Webb: Explain your thinking in an elevator pitch

Educators often ask, "Is there a difference between Bloom's revised taxonomy and DOK?" How would you reply?

The "elevator pitch"—summarize your key points in less than one minute, the length of an elevator ride.

In an alignment study, reviewers classify and code test items for content and DOK level. In a classroom, educators want to determine the complexity of learning activities so they can plan for instruction and assessment. Identifying the *intended* DOK level of a task helps teachers to determine what concepts and skills students need to learn in order to successfully complete a task. For example, if students are learning new vocabulary terms, they might need to know how to use a dictionary or learn how to use language structure (roots, prefixes, and suffixes) to determine word meaning (DOK 1). After memorizing definitions of words, students might be asked to use the context of a sentence or paragraph to determine which meaning of a word is intended (DOK 2). For vocabulary terms that represent concepts (photosynthesis, assertion, mathematical representation, etc.), students might be asked to use evidence and observations to support interpretations of those concepts (DOK 3).

Let's look at a few classroom examples that have been analyzed for the intended DOK level, based on the mental processing required to complete the task (Table 1.3). After studying and discussing the examples, complete the table with your analysis of each task example.

To check your understanding after completing Table 1.3, see Appendix A, pp. 87–88. Then reflect on your current understanding of differences between DOK levels and any new insights you've gained.

Activity 1.3: Analyzing the intended Depth of Knowledge (DOK) levels of learning or assessment tasks by completing the table

Read each sample task below and underline a few key words to help you decide whether you think it requires DOK 1, 2 3, or 4 thinking. Then discuss interpretations with colleagues and provide your agreed-upon reasoning for the intended DOK level for each task. There are some tricky descriptions that might fool you, so read carefully!

Table 1.3. Analyzing the Intended DOK Levels of Learning or Assessment Tasks

Task Examples	Intended DOK Level	What mental processing is called upon to complete the task?
1. Listen to or read an article about holidays. Then present information describing some of the customs and traditions of the place you read about.	1	The final product for "presenting" is not specified, so it may not be a full summary (DOK 2). "Presenting information" is likely to be a list of explicit facts or bullet points or perhaps a drawing (DOK 1). This task requires little or no analysis nor organization of ideas.
2. Create step-by-step instructions on how to draw a simple closed figure using a protractor and ruler. You must include the angles and the exact measurement of the lines in millimeters and centimeters. Make sure to use proper math terminology in your instructions.	2	Summarizing steps to complete a routine task generally does not require deep thinking. Students use prior knowledge of angles, measurement tools, and terms (DOK 1) to create organized, step-by-step instructions (DOK 2).
3. Write or retell a story we have read from another character's point of view.	3	The final product requires analyzing the same storyline from a different perspective or point of view (POV). To do this, students must analyze the chosen character's motivations, actions, interactions, and words. These story details are used to support interpretations of the different POV (DOK 3).
4. View several videos of "The Star-Spangled Banner" from educationally respected websites (e.g., History Channel, Smithsonian Institute, or *History Detectives* on PBS). Identify what depictions are more and less prevalent among the sites' videos. Describe how the videos differ. Draw conclusions as to why the different organizations might highlight different aspects of our national anthem.	4	Students must investigate multiple sources and analyze how (format used) and why (each author's POV) the same information might be presented differently. This task might also require investigating each organization's mission. Conclusions are supported with evidence from multiple sources. (DOK 4)
5. Create a booklet of ______. Include illustrations, a description of attributes, and other identifiable information for each example.	Intended DOK?	Your Reasoning . . .
6. Compare and contrast two novels written in about the same time period and determine which version is the most historically accurate. Use evidence cited in the texts and other sources to support your conclusions.		
7. Explain the difference between a ratio and a proportion. Provide examples and non-examples of each to support your explanation.		
8. Evaluate the historical accuracy of a novel you have read. Compare evidence in the text to historical facts from the same place and time period to support your conclusions		
9. Invent a new word. Include its definition, root, affix, part of speech, synonyms, antonyms, an example, a sentence using the word, and the context in which you believe the word would be understood.		

(*continued*)

Table 1.3. (*continued*)

Task Examples	Intended DOK Level	What mental processing is called upon to complete the task?
10. Compose an original poem using one of the forms or genres we have studied. Include an analysis of the poem's construction using appropriate terminology and domain-specific language.		
11. Read short biographical sketches of authors who have written in a specific genre category. Illustrate or report on what elements they have in common.		
12. Select one of the Van Gogh paintings at https://www.vangoghmuseum.nl/en/collection. Create an implicit statement about what you see, such as describing the style or mood. Then use visual evidence to support your interpretations, such as how it portrays peacefulness, sadness, despair, or power.		
13. Make a table showing the advantages and disadvantages of _____(any topic).		
14. Two friends were arguing about the best seat in the movie theater. One of them had heard that it is best to sit so that the angle formed by the line of sight between the left and right sides of the screen is 30 degrees. John believes there is only one seat in the theater that meets this criterion. Amy argues there is more than one place where the viewing angle is 30 degrees. Decide who is correct and provide supporting mathematical evidence.		
15. Create a game that will teach your classmates about ________. Include important facts, concepts, and related images. Provide a set of directions with your game.		
16. Create a model of one system of the human body. Label each organ/part of the body system, describing how the parts of the system work together. Be prepared to answer questions about what might be the short- and longer-term result if a particular part malfunctions or there is an injury to the system.		
17. Investigate how water pollution affects the fishing industry and which states are most significantly impacted. Create a presentation to share your analysis of the impact of pollution on fishing in these states using specific examples.		

Activity 1.4: Time to reflect

Has your understanding of DOK or distinctions among the four DOK levels changed or been refined in some way? Have you gained any new insights? What questions do you still have?

BUILDING ON BLOOM AND WEBB: CREATING THE HESS COGNITIVE RIGOR MATRICES

The Hess Cognitive Rigor Matrices (CRMs) are now used throughout the United States and in dozens of countries around the world to assist educators in applying what cognitive demand might look like in the classroom and to design or analyze test items and performance-based tasks. Content-specific descriptors in each of the CRMs can be used to categorize and plan for various levels of mental processing required to respond to assessment questions and learning tasks. From schools to testing companies, the CRMs have been used for professional learning activities, curriculum and assessment work, and test item development. So how were the Hess Cognitive Rigor Matrices created?

Remember that flight home, in 2005, when I was contemplating how Bloom and Webb were (or were not) related? I sketched a blank matrix template, putting Bloom's six thinking levels along the vertical axis and the four DOK levels across the top (Table 1.4). At first, I thought maybe descriptors of Bloom's levels of "Remember" and "Understand" would line up nicely with DOK 1, and descriptors for "Apply" might equate with DOK 2. I soon discovered this assumption was wrong. Drawing from Webb's 2002 work, I began to populate the cells of the draft matrix, with reading and writing DOK-level descriptors. I soon realized that there were curricular examples in language arts at every DOK level for almost every cell in my new matrix. When I saw that this approach was working well for language arts, I tried aligning a few mathematics and science DOK descriptors with each level of Bloom. Eureka! My idea of a cognitive rigor matrix was born. It was becoming clear to me that what we've thought of as "higher order" verbs and thinking levels—analyzing, evaluating, and creating—did not always result in learning tasks requiring deep understanding or strategic thinking.

As I worked on the evolving matrix, I still had to resolve what to put in the cells at the lower DOK levels for "Evaluate" and at the upper DOK levels for "Remember." As I thought more about describing "Remember" in terms of *depth*, it made no sense to put anything under DOK 2, 3, or 4. You either know something or you don't. It's as simple as that. Those cells were purposely left blank.

Deciding what to put in the row for "Evaluate" under DOK 1 and DOK 2 was perplexing. What do you call it when you evaluate something—state an opinion or try to make an argument—and have no supporting evidence, no elaboration, and cite no source? The answer came as a flashback from my past. These were "UGs." I frequently saw this notation on the early papers that I wrote while in graduate school. If my professor put an "UG" in the margin, it meant that I had an unsubstantiated (unsupported) generalization; I had stated an opinion, claim, or a "truth" but provided no credible support for it. An UG sent you back to find a source to back up your claims or ideas.

Throughout this development process, I came to better understand that deeper learning and thinking was not simply about verbs, taxonomies, complex texts, or what we have generally accepted as "higher-order" thinking. There was a significant difference between "analysis lite" (DOK 1 or DOK 2) and deeper analysis of a topic or concept (DOK 3 or DOK 4).

EXPANDING DOK TO MORE CONTENT AREAS

Webb's early work applied DOK in four core content areas, so it made sense to design my first CRM prototypes for English Language Arts (ELA)-social studies and mathematics-science. At that time, I also wrote a little paper, "Exploring Cognitive Demand in Instruction and Assessment" (Hess, 2005), about examining different complexity models and my decision to merge the Bloom and Webb models to create the matrices. The paper was posted and widely read. As my understanding of cognitive science grew, I saw the need for each content domain to have its unique schema represented in a single rigor matrix. My first two CRMs evolved into four separate CRMs: reading/

Table 1.4. Building a Cognitive Rigor Matrix to Describe Increasing Levels of Complexity

Bloom	DOK 1	DOK 2	DOK 3	DOK 4
Remember	Recall a fact, detail, or term.	I wondered, "does anything go here?"		
Understand	Identify literary elements.	Summarize a text.	Identify theme or point of view.	
Apply	Apply rules of editing.	Use context to determine meaning.		Illustrate how multiple themes are interrelated.
Analyze	Identify information in a text feature.	Compare characters.		
Evaluate	What goes here? Is this an opinion without any supporting evidence? UGs = Unsupported Generalizations		Citing evidence, develop a logical argument for conjectures.	
Create	Brainstorm ideas on a topic.			Synthesize ideas across sources.

listening, math/science, writing/speaking, and social studies/humanities, as I continued to integrate new descriptors from other models to all of them. Now, on a single page, a school could use DOK descriptors in the CRMs to visually map the range of cognitive rigor addressed in their local curriculum and assessments for each core content area. For schools still using Bloom, there were entry points to each DOK level using Bloom's levels.

When I got questions about what DOK might look like in other content areas, I explored different approaches for fine arts, health/physical education, world languages, and career and technical education. Up to this point, the CRMs integrated Bloom levels with DOK levels. However, I found that while DOK descriptions might work in every content area, some content areas did not readily lend themselves to using Bloom. I could have simply used four DOK levels for these matrices, but I wanted "categories" familiar to teachers in each of these disciplines. Below is a brief description of Hess CRMs in other subject areas that did not easily integrate Bloom with DOK. (All of the Hess CRMs can be found in Appendix B or downloaded at https://www.karin-hess.com/cognitive-rigor-and-dok. Spanish versions are also available at this link.)

The Hess CRM for Fine Arts was created while I was working with three states (Maryland, Rhode Island, and Kentucky) in the development of their state standards and assessments for visual arts, music, dance, and theater. Arts educators helped me to identify four common arts practices that could integrate with DOK descriptors: critique, creative expression and production, historical/social/cultural context, and perceiving and performing. This CRM represents my interpretation of DOK when applied to fine arts practices, drawing upon examples from fine arts learning activities and standards across many states.

The Hess CRM for Health and Physical Education was created through my work with several K–12 school faculties. As with fine arts, health and physical education teachers struggled to see how DOK or Bloom applied to their curriculums. For this CRM, I developed DOK descriptors drawn from the outcomes in the National Physical Education Standards (National Association for Sport and Physical Education, 2004; Society of Health and Physical Education, 2024) and connected them with the cognitive categories from Porter and Smithson's Survey of Enacted Curriculum SEC (2001), a survey tool used to analyze local teaching practices in relation to content standards. The SEC categories vary slightly by content area. I decided that the science categories of memorize, communicate understanding, perform procedures, apply concepts, and analyze information could generally be applied to categorize health and physical education outcomes and then generated examples for each DOK level.

The Hess CRM for World Languages was created with world language teacher-coaches Rachel Gilbert and Amy Flynn, who helped me identify five broad common expectations consistent with modes of communication, national standards, and English Language Learner (ELL) assessment descriptors. Curricular examples in world language courses were used to develop the DOK level descriptors.

The Hess CRM for Career and Technical Education closely resembles descriptors in the math-science CRM, which was being used by many career and technical education (CTE) teachers at the time this was developed. Kirsten Soroko, Director of Personalized Learning and Growth at Pinkerton Academy in Derry, New Hampshire, helped me to gather assessment examples from a variety of CTE courses (construction trades, graphic arts, computer science, etc.) in order to develop draft DOK descriptors. Later we elicited feedback from CTE teachers in several career and technical centers to refine DOK descriptors applicable to CTE courses.

COGNITIVE RIGOR, COGNITIVE DEMAND, AND DOK

Cognitive demand is the potential range of mental processing required to complete a task within a specific context or scenario. Is the student practicing a skill in isolation or perhaps applying a combination of skills and concepts to investigate open-ended problems? Thinking at each DOK level requires a different level of cognitive demand or mental processing and engagement with the content. Hess and colleagues (2009) clarified the connections between DOK (mental processing and engagement) and cognitive rigor in this often-quoted description: "Cognitive rigor is a combination of the complexity of the content, the cognitive engagement with the content, and the scope of the planned learning activity."

Cognitive rigor is more than simply identifying DOK levels of tasks or test questions. It's connecting the intended purpose of the learning task with how students will engage with content.

Table 1.5 illustrates connections among different learning purposes and mental processing generally associated with each DOK level, regardless of content area or grade level. The DOK examples in the far-right column describe learning activities for a grade 3 classroom, featured in the PBLWorks video clip, "Tiny House Project." The learning goal for this series of lessons might be stated as: "Students will apply their knowledge of measurement concepts and opinion writing to design, build, and present a model of a tiny house that meets given specicfications."

View the grade 3 video, "Tiny House Project," at https://www.pblworks.org/video-tiny-house-project. Complete Table 1.5 by creating your own classroom example.

VALIDATING USES OF THE HESS COGNITIVE RIGOR MATRICES

The content-specific Hess CRMs describe a range of cognitively demanding tasks, from the least to the most complex, providing educators with a more sophisticated lens to systematically guide planning and development of tasks that increase in complexity. Descriptors in the Hess CRMs offer a common language for analyzing the cognitive demand of assessments, units of study, and learning tasks. Often these analyses have led to refinements in classroom questioning, the redesign of learning tasks, and the development of high-quality assessments. Numerous research studies have successfully used or adapted the matrices to examine everything from curriculum implementation to teachers' capacity to design rigorous tasks. Below are a few examples of how the matrices have been used to answer rigor-related research questions.

- In 2007–2008, the math and reading CRMs were used by The Standards Company to conduct a large-scale analysis of assignments given to students in Oklahoma and Nevada over a 3-month time period (Hess et al., 2009). Work samples of homework

Table 1.5. Creating a Flow of Learning and Assessment Tasks for Different DOK Levels

DOK Level and Purpose	Mental processing (How students engage with content)	What students *could be* doing Stated as success criteria: I can . . .	A content-specific example for grade 3	Create at least one example for your classroom. Circle the mental processing used.
1 Acquire a Foundation	Memorize facts, definitions, details. Reproduce/perform routine skills and procedures. Retrieve, recall, or locate information.	• Follow specific steps to complete routine tasks or use tools, resources. • Practice using a standard algorithm or routine operation. • Locate/recall/memorize facts, dates, terms, details. • Match/identify definitions. • Recite/paraphrase definitions, principles.	Students listen to a structural engineer and discuss how to create blueprints. They work at different stations to acquire vocabulary and skills in finding area and perimeter, how to write an opinion, and how to gather information through interviewing.	
2 Use, Connect, and Conceptualize	Describe or explain relationships. Apply under-lying conceptual understanding. Make basic inferences	• Summarize key ideas (one text, one event); create concept map or timeline. • Explain relationships: compare-contrast, if-then. • Record, graph, organize observations. • Select and use a strategy or tool for specific task. • Sort or classify based on given criteria; predict.	As a class, students build schema about how blueprints and models are constructed to meet different specifications and "practice" strategies for effective presentations.	
3 Deepen and Construct Meaning	Reason abstractly and metacognitively. Solve nonroutine problems. Develop evaluative or argumentative claims on a topic. Transfer prior learning to new situations.	• Uncover relevant, accurate, credible information. • Use criteria/evidence to develop or evaluate reports, arguments, narratives. • Create models, metaphors. • Conduct investigations; solve nonroutine problems. • Self-assess; apply feedback. • Make connections to Big Ideas/ Essential Questions.	Groups plan and build prototypes of model houses. They use a peer feedback protocol.	
4 Extend, Transfer, and Broaden Meaning	Reason abstractly and metacognitively. Gather, analyze, and synthesize information across sources to solve nonroutine problems. Transfer prior learning to novel/real-world situations.	• Raise novel questions; investigate real-world issues. • Design and conduct project, research, investigation. • Draw from multiple sources to analyze or evaluate solutions or alternatives. • Create authentic products. • Create a complex model. • Initiate self-assessments. • Develop broad insights linked to Big Ideas/Essential Questions.	Feedback is used to modify designs and develop opinion pieces to persuade clients to buy their house plan. Real-world connections are made with why people build tiny houses.	

assignments, tests, quizzes, and so forth were collected and analyzed to develop density plots that visually described the level of complexity (or actually the lack of complexity) in most of the work assigned to students during that time.

- An action research study (Banner, 2016) sought to determine how instructional rigor was understood by core subject middle school teachers in Connecticut. The Hess (2013) matrix was used with an implementation rigor rubric and a three-step planning process as a framework for positively impacting the teachers' capacity to design and implement rigorous tasks. Teachers reported that the Hess matrix, used in conjunction with collaborative planning and the implementation rubric, positively impacted their thinking and their capacity to design rigorous tasks, which was corroborated by the classroom observations.
- A research study (Nelson & Zayed, 2019) adapted the Hess CRM for writing as a means of determining the emphasis placed on each of its intersections in teaching of nonfiction essay writing in Saudi Arabia. Researchers used findings to identify ways to enhance learning opportunities and writing skills for students in an essay-writing course.
- In a study using Webb's DOK alignment protocols to compare complex thinking required by the elementary New Jersey Student Learning Standards and past New Jersey Curriculum Standards, one conclusion stated, "The replication of this study or related studies can be conducted utilizing Hess's Cognitive Rigor Matrix. . . . further research can be done to analyze the assessed curriculum through conceptual framework such as Hess's Cognitive Rigor Matrix . . . or Webb's Depth of Knowledge" (Fitzhugh, 2019, p. 146).

SUMMING UP

There have always been a variety of thinking models available to educators; however, all are not equally effective for planning and assessing learning at its deepest levels. Both Bloom and Webb originally developed models for analyzing test items. Over the years, their ideas have been expanded upon to guide K–12 instruction and assessment. The content-specific cognitive rigor matrices draw upon the unique perspectives of Bloom, Webb, and others, while attempting to maintain a high level of fidelity with the original models.

In my work examining cognitive rigor, I've found the DOK framework clear enough for me to examine and compare other models and flexible enough to see multiple uses. So, is DOK the "be-all and end-all" of complexity models? Coined by Shakespeare in *Macbeth*, that phrase is used today to mean the whole thing, the last word, something that is so entirely suitable as to eliminate the need for a search for an alternative. No, I don't think DOK is the "be-all and end-all" of complexity models. But the underlying meaning, clarity, and intent of each DOK level makes me think of it as the "MVP" of complexity models, a lens that is

- **Meaningful** enough to align measurement tasks or instructional activities with the intended purpose(s);
- **Valid** in describing what cognitive rigor, deeper understanding, and learning transfer actually look like; and
- **Practical** enough for teachers in the classroom to find it useful.

On a somewhat humorous side note, my first article describing the Hess Cognitive Rigor Matrix was rejected by a major educational publication, stating that "it is too complicated for teachers to understand and use." Now it's used by educators in more than 120 countries! Perseverance paid off.

Misconceptions, Misinterpretations, and Myths—Oh, My!

> **Key Questions Explored in Module 2:**
> - Can *all* students—meaning all ages, all grade levels, all ability levels—actually engage in complex work?
> - Are there specific verbs or question prompts that are always associated with each DOK level?
> - Is DOK intended to be used as a taxonomy or perhaps as a learning progression?

Increasing interest and applications of DOK are now widespread, yet many misconceptions about DOK still abound. Over the years, I've read numerous books and articles describing depth of knowledge and how to apply it. It seems that the one thing all of them get right is that the original idea of a depth of knowledge framework began with Norman Webb's work with alignment studies and that there are four DOK levels. But when I look for specific applications or examples of each DOK level, I see some that in my opinion are "spot on," while others are promoting incorrect information. For example, there might be a mixture of accurate and not-so-accurate examples given for question prompts at different DOK levels, with DOK 2 and DOK 3 being the most confused. Or there might be accurate information followed by a visual image of a verb wheel matching the levels of Bloom's taxonomy with DOK levels.

It's time to debunk the myths! Let's begin by reflecting on your current understanding.

WHAT IS YOUR CURRENT UNDERSTANDING OF DOK?

Use the anticipation guide in Activity 2.1 as a preassessment to reflect on your understanding right now. Start by reading each statement about DOK. Decide whether you disagree (D) or agree (A). Indicate by placing an X to the left of each statement under D or A. In the middle column, explain why you disagree or agree *right now*. After working through the module—reading about, viewing, or discussing each misconception—make notes (to the far right) as to whether your opinion or understandings have changed and explain your revised reasoning. (Each explanation requires supporting evidence—citing texts, research, observed evidence, etc.)

DEBUNKING SEVEN OF THE MOST COMMON MISCONCEPTIONS

After you've completed the preassessment individually, you have several options: (1) read about each misconception on your own, (2) read and discuss the information about each misconception with peers, or (3) create a jigsaw activity by dividing into seven groups, with each group discussing a different misconception and then sharing conclusions with the whole group. After reading, viewing, or discussing the seven misconceptions, return to the anticipation guide at the beginning of the module and complete step 3—describe how your thinking has been clarified, revised, or changed.

⊘ Misconception 1: All students aren't able to think deeply, or all students shouldn't need scaffolding and support in order to think deeply and complete complex tasks.

Highly creative and productive adults usually seek support to complete complex tasks with models and

Activity 2.1 Pre-Post Self-Assessment. (1) Read each statement in the self-assessment, decide whether you agree or disagree, and (2) explain why. After completing the module, (3) explain whether your thinking has changed or been clarified.

D Disagree	A Agree	STEP 1: Do you agree/disagree (X) with each statement below? If you're not sure, go with your gut feeling right now.	STEP 2: Explain your thinking *right now* (drawing on your background knowledge or supporting evidence).	STEP 3: After completing the module, *has your thinking changed or been confirmed*? What sources/evidence help to explain your thinking now?
		1. All students can think deeply and engage in complex work.		
		2. DOK level is influenced by a student's grade level or ability to complete tasks independently.		
		3. Collaboration does *not* decrease the DOK level of a task.		
		4. Webb's DOK Framework is designed to be a taxonomy, like Bloom's taxonomy.		
		5. Specific verbs for each DOK level can be used to plan lessons or write test questions.		
		6. DOK levels are influenced by the difficulty of a task, or the amount of time or effort required to complete it.		
		7. All DOK levels can be assessed with multiple-choice questions.		
		8. Anyone, of any ability level, taking on a complex challenge can benefit from scaffolding.		
		9. Only higher-order verbs of Bloom's taxonomy (analyze, evaluate, create) lead to deep understanding.		
		10. Completing multistep tasks or reading complex texts are *not* indicators of higher DOK levels.		
		11. DOK levels from 1 to 4 represent learning progressions.		
		12. Providing scaffolding for a task decreases complexity.		

mentors, and by working through and refining their ideas with feedback from others. When adults take on complex challenges, they benefit from scaffolding. The same is true for students—even the highest-performing students. Regardless of innate ability, all students can think deeply. It's up to us to strategically scaffold learning so that students can access complex content or apply complex procedures, moving learning from foundational to conceptual to deeper understanding.

- Vygotsky's (1978) concept of the zone of proximal development (ZPD) represents a challenge just beyond a student's current level of independent mastery. Through social interactions (e.g., discourse, collaborative problem-solving), gaps in understanding can be bridged and learning moves forward.
- Learning how to tackle a complex task with others is important to be able to produce similar high-quality products on their own. Research suggests that collaboration does *not* reduce the complexity of a task; it allows students to explore topics and ideas more quickly and more deeply in a low-stakes environment (Hess & Gong, 2014).
- Scaffolding is not the same as making modifications to the original task, which usually changes what students are being asked to do, thus reducing the DOK level. Scaffolding can break complex tasks down into more meaningful parts, without changing the intended DOK level. A pilot study in Georgia (Hess et al., 2008) with over 2,000 special education students, grades 5–8, explored various ways to structure reading and mathematics questions with scaffolding that made the items more accessible while not changing the constructs being assessed. Using questions from the state's grade-level assessment test items and grade-level reading passages, test questions were presented differently. For example, reading questions were reordered from basic questions to more complex and embedded within the passages (chunking the text), rather than all questions listed at the end of the passage. Mathematics test questions were grouped by content domain (e.g., all of the operations questions, then data questions, then geometry questions). Both of these strategies were found to support students in retrieving what they actually had learned without taxing their executive functioning to the point of them giving up and not completing the test. In one-on-one interviews with students after finishing the tests, an overwhelming number of students said they felt they did well. These students may not have gotten all questions correct, but when students have confidence, they are more likely to access what is stored in their memories and answer all of the test questions. Thus, the structure of tasks and test questions can have a positive effect on all students demonstrating what they have learned.
- Students need multiple opportunities to successfully engage with complex tasks; therefore, educators must be intentional about how they balance the complexity of the content with the ways that students engage with it. Bloom (1968) referenced the need for providing time and support in his classic article "Learning for Mastery," saying that when given sufficient time and appropriate types of help, 95% of students can learn a subject up to a high level of mastery.

In summary, several key things are needed for all students to think deeply and accomplish complex tasks. First and foremost, educators need to adopt a belief that all students *can* do this type of work, regardless of grade level or innate ability. Tasks should be structured for optimal access and multiple ways to respond. Collaboration that encourages students to work through ideas with others first and oral language and discourse that uncovers what thinking and reasoning actually looks and sounds like can support deeper learning for every student.

Watch Part 3 of Karin's Master Class on applying cognitive rigor, "Are Your Students Thinking Deeply, or Just Working Harder?"
Dr. Hess describes scaffolding strategies at https://youtu.be/WYSYWe2OvcM.

Misconception 2: DOK levels are a taxonomy, or DOK levels represent learning progressions.

Bloom's original taxonomy (Bloom, 1956) and the revised Bloom's taxonomy (Anderson et al., 2001) were both conceived to be a hierarchy describing lower to higher levels of thinking. The goal was to get students thinking at the highest levels. In a taxonomy, "lower order" thinking is often devalued.

- **Webb's DOK framework was not intended to be used as a taxonomy** (Webb et al., 2023). If DOK was a taxonomy, then our goal would be to have students working with content at the deepest levels of engagement (DOK 3 and DOK 4) most of the time. As an instructional approach, this is not realistic and would not be supportive of all learners. A DOK taxonomy implies that extended thinking (DOK 4) is more valued than strategic thinking (DOK 3); that strategic thinking is better than conceptual understanding (DOK2); and that it is better than recall of foundational/surface knowledge (DOK 1). This view devalues the role of foundational and conceptual understanding in laying the groundwork for deeper thinking. DOK levels should be seen as nominative; they name—or describe—the complexity of student engagement required by the learning expectation. Learning expectations can be at any DOK level. Sometimes students are working at a foundational level to acquire new terms, rules, and skills. Sometimes they are building conceptual understanding, and at other times they may be applying what they've learned to novel situations through problem-solving or research. Cognitive rigor and DOK levels represent a balance of how a learner acquires and uses what was learned in increasingly more complex ways. A better approach is to set learning expectations across the range of DOK levels—which leads us to the next, and sometimes confusing, connection between DOK and learning progressions.
- **DOK levels are not intended to describe simple to complex learning progressions** (Webb et al., 2023); however, it's easy to see how one might interpret increasing DOK levels as a learning progression. First, let's clarify the differences. True learning progressions (LPs) are content-specific, developed from empirical research, and supported with instruction. LPs describe how most students typically build expertise *over extended periods of time,* demonstrating novice to expert performance. Like DOK levels, they describe learning that is not grade level–specific. Most LP research suggests that learning begins with broad conceptual understanding (DOK 2), then moves to basic practice (DOK 1). For example, students are taught through hands-on experiences the concepts of joining together or equivalence before the + and = signs are introduced. Then students might practice routine addition problems, first with manipulatives, then with numbers—some problems with one missing addend, and others changing the order of missing addends (all DOK 1). Eventually, routine story problems applying addition (DOK 2) are introduced and practiced. Multiple strategies for solving addition problems in varied contexts might also be practiced at this time (a combination of DOK 1 and 2) before students solve open-ended, problem-solving tasks applying addition (DOK 3). I might describe this "sequence" as: DOK 2–1–1–2–1–2–3–3. Learning progressions are more cyclical than sequential because the "learning" pathway expands knowledge and skills. They are more like building mental maps (schemas) organized around big ideas than creating a direct route to a short-term destination.

In summary, DOK is neither a taxonomy nor intended to be used as a simple learning progression. Learning progressions are often cyclical and more complex than a simple DOK 1 to DOK 4 sequencing of tasks. However, a DOK mindset can be used to analyze the range and complexity of learning expectations described in a learning progression or to analyze student work samples to better understand how learning develops over time, along a continuum. One strategy researchers use to develop learning progressions is by analyzing student work samples. (See Module 6 for an explanation of how Tool 12, Student Work Analysis, is used to analyze student work along a continuum and provide differentiated support.)

To make connections between DOK and learning progressions, you can analyze the stages of existing learning progressions using a DOK lens. Two documents synthesizing the research underlying content to be learned in the Common Core Standards (2010a, 2010b) in mathematics (Hess & Kearns, 2010) and English language arts (Hess & Kearns, 2011) break content standards into "chunks" that illustrate increased depth, breadth, and complexity along hypothetical learning progressions. Learning progressions are always considered hypothetical until they are tested and refined by examining student work samples.

Table 2.1 illustrates one strand of a language arts LP for reading comprehension in the left-hand column. Comprehending literary texts is the "unifying big idea" (or competency statement) for this LP, with a list of grades 5 and 6 supporting Common Core standards in English language arts that align with each performance indicator. The Hess CRM for Reading was used to identify one or more *intended* DOK levels in the right column for each performance indicator in the learning progression.

Activity 2.2: Examine and reflect

Study the sample learning progression in the left column of Table 2.1 and the DOK analysis of each performance indicator (M.RL.a–g) on the right. What connections can you make about learning progressions and DOK?

Misconception 3: Verb wheels, specific verb lists, and Bloom's taxonomy levels can be aligned with specific DOK levels.

Perhaps you've seen—or tried to use—a widely circulated image of a wheel divided into four DOK sections, with verb lists in each section. For years, I've called this "The DOK Wheel of Misfortune"—it implies that you can spin the wheel, pick a verb, and voilà! Your students will be thinking deeply. If you look closely, you will see some of the same verbs appearing in more than one DOK section. That is your first red flag about verbs determining complexity levels. Since I am frequently asked about the DOK wheel, it's worth stating that neither Norman Webb nor I created it. I think it may have been derived from an earlier Bloom's taxonomy wheel that appeared in Barbara Clark's book *Growing Up Gifted* (1983, p. 222). In Clark's book, this wheel had verbs in each of the sections that represented levels of Bloom's taxonomy. Clark used the Bloom wheel to make the insightful case that rather than a linear hierarchy, the taxonomy should be viewed as a repeating cycle; the highest levels of thinking produce new insights and products that lead to a need to go back to lower levels of Bloom and further develop the knowledge base. That in turn leads to much deeper understanding in the next learning cycle.

The DOK wheel and side-by-side images equating DOK levels with levels of Bloom's taxonomy imply connections between the two models that really don't exist. Here is what we know about using verbs as the primary indicator of task complexity or deeper thinking:

- Verbs describe types of thinking, not depth of understanding.
- Verbs are generic, void of content. Thinking and accessing information stored in long-term memory is domain specific, not simply generic mental processing. For example, analyzing a literary text requires a different schema and thought processes than analyzing a musical composition or experimental design.
- DOK levels are not limited to specific verbs.
- The more complex a task is (by DOK level), the more types of thinking (more verbs) will be needed to successfully complete it.

In summary, it's actually what comes after the verb—the content—and the cognitive engagement with that content that determines overall complexity of a task. Table 2.2 illustrates tasks using the same verb "describe," which is often associated with lower-level thinking. Explanations of the mental processing required to complete each task are also included for tasks at each DOK level.

Misconception 4: DOK is about greater effort, time, or difficulty—tasks just getting harder.

Somewhere in our collective educational pasts, we got the idea that "rigorous" means that something is

Table 2.1. Analyzing DOK Levels Within a Learning Progression

Sample Reading Comprehension Learning Progression, Grades 5–6 (Hess & Kearns, 2011, p. 31)	**Analyzing DOK Levels of Performance Indicators** Coding for LP performance indicators is M (middle school) RL (Reading Literary) Texts. Complexity increases from a to g.
Coding below each LP Indictor represents Common Core ELA Standards grades 5 and 6 Grades 5–6 Comprehend Literary texts by . . .	**Grades 5–6 Learning Progression Progress Indicators** (Skills and concepts from either grade's standards address each progress indicator.)
M.RL.a flexibly using strategies to derive meaning form a variety of texts 5.RF-4c; 5.RL-4; 5.L-4, 5a, 5c 6.RL-4; 6.L-4, 5	**M.RL.a** • Choose an appropriate strategy for a specific purpose and perform it—**DOK 2**
M.RL.b using evidence from the text to support interpretations, inferences, or conclusions (e.g., character or plot development, point of view) 5.RL-1, 6 6.RL-1, 3, 6	**M.RL.b** • Use text evidence to support inferences—**DOK 2** • Use text evidence to support conclusions—**DOK 3**
M.RL.c summarizing and interpreting purpose or central ideas to derive a theme 5.RL.2 6.RL-2	**M.RL.c** • Summarize central ideas—**DOK 2** • Derive purpose or theme—**DOK 3**
M.RL.d comparing literary elements (e.g., character, setting, plot/subplots) within or across texts 5.RL-3, 9	**M.RL.d** • Compare literary elements within texts—**DOK 2** • Compare literary elements across texts—**DOK 4**
M.RL.e analyzing texts according to text structure, genre features, or author's style 5.RL-5, 6, 7, 9 6.RL-5, 9	**M.RL.e** • Analyze text structure, genre features—**DOK 2 or 3** • Analyze author's style—**DOK 3**
M.RL.f identifying and describing how the narrative point of view influences the reader's interpretation 5.RL-6 6.RL-6	**M.RL.f** • Identify narrator point of view—**DOK 1** • Describe how point of view influences interpretation—**DOK 3**
M.RL.g applying aspects of author's craft (e.g., literary devices) when analyzing literary elements, style, or mood within or across texts 5.RL-4, 6, 7, 9; L-4, 5a 6.RL-4, 6, 7, 9; 6.L-5a	**M.RL.g** • Apply authors craft when analyzing literary devices within texts—**DOK 3** • Apply author's craft when analyzing element style or mood across texts—**DOK 4**

Table 2.2. Increasing Task Complexity Using the Same Verb

VERB	SAMPLE TASK	DOK	EXPLANATION OF MENTAL PROCESSING REQUIRED
Describe	Describe the information presented in this graph or a table.	1	This requires recalling how graphs/tables are constructed and reading the title and axes. Students are not working with the data but simply describing what the data represent. There is one correct answer.
Describe	Describe how these situations/scenarios are alike or different.	2	Students make connections by reading the entire text and looking for explicit relevant examples that can be compared and contrasted. There is a correct answer, although different examples could be used.
Describe	Describe the data or text evidence that supports your solution, your reasoning, or your conclusions about the effects of this phenomenon.	3	This requires articulating how the analysis of evidence influenced reasoning to arrive at a solution or conclusion, or to justify that a solution is viable. Different evidence, different approaches to the task, and the degree to which the analysis of evidence is of high quality are used to evaluate the "correctness" of the student's response.
Describe	Describe varying perspectives on this phenomenon using supporting scientific evidence, and identify the most significant effects it might have on the planet in 100 years.	4	This requires not only an analysis of relevant evidence, but evidence coming from multiple sources. It also requires a deep understanding of the content (a phenomenon) and justification of criteria used to determine and predict "significant" effects. There is more than one possible correct answer. As with DOK 3, the credibility of evidence and the degree to which the analysis of evidence is of high quality and is used to explain differing perspectives contribute to evaluating the "correctness" of the student's response.

Source: Hess, 2018, p. 41; used with permission.

Activity 2.3: Practice Activity—*It's what comes after the verb!*

Complete the table below using a verb (other than "describe") with different content to illustrate all four DOK levels. Remember to describe the mental processes required to successfully complete each task.

Increasing Task Complexity Using the Same Verb

MY VERB	SAMPLE TASKS	DOK	EXPLANATION of MENTAL PROCESSING REQUIRED
		1	This requires recalling, locating, or reproducing . . . There is a correct answer.
		2	Students make connections or decisions by . . . There is a correct answer.
		3	This requires reasoning, planning, and evidence: Different evidence, different approaches to the task, and the degree to which the use of evidence is of high quality are used to evaluate the "correctness" of the student's response.
		4	This requires reasoning and evidence drawn from more than one source or complete development of an original product. The credibility and relevant use of evidence to support themes, claims, or unifying ideas is used to evaluate the "correctness" of the student's response.

really hard to do, requires a lot of effort, or takes a lot more time. Many dictionaries define "rigor" with synonyms like inflexible, hard, or rigid. Cognitive rigor is the opposite—it's flexible thinking, seeing multiple possibilities, approaches, or perspectives. To uncover multiple perspectives or approaches to a problem means to understand concepts deeply and apply them broadly. Tasks we learn as a beginner (e.g., skiing, decoding words, using mathematical formulas) may seem difficult or time-consuming at first. Practicing the routines to acquire new skills makes them easier and more automatic, but the DOK level doesn't change with practice. Routinely applying a mathematical formula is always DOK 1; it just gets easier with practice. A more complex task (DOK 3 or 4) requires students to apply learned skills and concepts in novel or unfamiliar situations. This is similar to athletic teams learning and practicing skills (dribbling, shooting, passing, etc.) before they apply them in a variety of ways in different game situations.

In summary, DOK is about engagement and the mental processing needed to complete the task, not how hard it is or how much time or effort is needed.

⊘ Misconception 5: All DOK levels can be assessed with a multiple-choice question.

Think about it. This claim doesn't make sense when you consider the level of engagement with content that is required by DOK 3– and DOK 4–type tasks (conducting investigations, researching, etc.), which are best assessed using constructed-response questions, performance tasks, or extended projects. To be clear, DOK 3 questions that focus on strategic thinking and reasoning can be assessed with multiple-choice questions. These items typically ask students to determine the author's purpose, identify text evidence or data that support a claim, interpret a complex graph or dataset, or identify flaws in an experimental design. When a student is selecting the "best" option on multiple-choice questions, such as locating supporting text evidence for a stated claim, the response yields a correct or incorrect answer, but it provides little insight to the teacher as to how a student applied concepts and reasoning to arrive at the answer or if the response is simply a result of guessing.

- A study published in the journal *Applied Measurement in Education* (cited in Arundel, 2024) found that students in grades 2–8 were more likely to rapidly guess at answers on low-stakes, computer-adaptive (multiple-choice) assessments in math and reading as the school day progressed, with the highest levels of guessing occurring later in the day.
- Some state assessments now use combinations of multiple-choice questions to address the additional processing of ideas required for deeper thinking (DOK 3) as an alternative to using constructed-response items. Unfortunately, getting the second part correct depends on getting the first part correct. If you cannot identify the theme in part 1, locating supporting evidence for the theme in part 2 is almost impossible, unless you are a lucky guesser! In theory, a combination of multiple-choice test questions may efficiently provide assessment information and speed in scoring, but it may also trip up students with limited executive functioning skills.
- DOK 4–type tasks typically require extended time, as well as extended thinking and reasoning, to process multiple sources of information. Because there is more content to analyze and more perspectives or possible solutions to consider, selected response items need to have distractors that are quite lengthy to read. Excessive reading load can become a "source of challenge" in the test item that is not related to what is actually being assessed, especially in mathematics assessments.

In summary, multiple-choice questions are easy to correct and can provide useful data for DOK 1– and DOK 2–type tasks (e.g., solving word problems in math). However, there are better assessment strategies to uncover what students do and do not actually understand when tasks are more complex. Usability of test data—especially formative uses—relies on being able to determine what students don't understand

and therefore, what instruction should occur next. Both the processing and the product of constructing an answer to a deeper/more rigorous question or task (DOK 3 or DOK 4) uncover understanding, and we've learned that students remember *and understand* answers they construct better than what they simply memorize. A helpful rule of thumb about assessing tasks at different DOK levels: Choose the assessment strategy and format that provides the most meaningful information, even if scoring (or grading) takes longer.

⊘ Misconception 6: Bloom's higher-order thinking levels always lead to deeper understanding.

Have you ever heard statements like, "I'm using higher-order thinking questions in my lesson. That means my students are learning at deeper levels"?

This is a very common misconception, and the reason why I originally created my matrices—to demonstrate that what we have generally thought of as "higher-order" thinking (analyzing, evaluating, and creating) might not always lead to deep understanding. For example, the Hess Cognitive Rigor Matrix for Math-Science illustrates a range of DOK levels for the skill of analysis: (DOK 1) retrieve information from a graph; (DOK 2) organize and order data; (DOK 3) draw conclusions using data, citing evidence; and (DOK 4) analyze multiple sources of evidence in datasets. All of these tasks involve important learning, but only some of them will demonstrate deep thinking. A creative "what if" writing assignment might be engaging or fun for students, but will it deepen their understanding? Fun and engaging is not a bad thing—hooking students on a personal level (emotional engagement) generally leads to deeper cognitive engagement later (Hess, 2023). Emotional engagement is not the same as cognitive engagement, which deepens understanding and builds mental schemas.

In summary, we can bust the myth that "understanding" and "application" activities only serve lower-order thinking when we can articulate task examples across a range of DOK levels 1–4, as illustrated in the cognitive rigor matrices. A range of thinking approaches is needed to achieve deeper thinking. To analyze content, learners must first *understand* the content at a deeper level (DOK 3–4). To evaluate content, learners must first analyze varying perspectives and components (DOK 3–4) and then *derive and apply* criteria for making judgments (DOK 3–4). To create new processes and products, learners must use skills to deepen their understanding, their application and analysis strategies, and their ability to evaluate options.

⊘ Misconception 7: Using multistep tasks, multiple resources, or complex texts will lead to deeper thinking.

I've sometimes heard people describe DOK levels in this way: One step means DOK 1, two steps mean DOK 2, three steps mean DOK 3, and so on. All multistep tasks are not created equal; many are actually learned routines with multiple steps. These include applying skills and rules that are important to know but that are still considered foundational learning (DOK 1). Think about long division. It can have many steps and can be hard to do at first, but it is still a routine operation done the same way every time. Now, contrast the long division assignment with researching a topic, which also has multiple steps. Here, students might begin by building some foundational knowledge (e.g., brainstorming what they know about a topic; learning new terms and vocabulary; conducting a keyword search—all DOK 1) and making connections between terms and concepts or examining cause-effect relationships (DOK 2). Then they might move to gathering data to help answer an issue-based question. The steps of this process may begin as routine but may later involve planning and strategic thinking to determine relevance and accuracy of information and to evaluate the validity of sources used. The number of steps is *not* the determining factor of cognitive rigor; it is the nonroutine nature of how one step might lead to decisions made about other steps in the process that deepens complexity and learning.

Likewise, does the number of texts read or the complexity of a text always lead to deeper understanding and higher DOK levels? I would say that the task expectations and the level of engagement needed with the text to complete the task are as important as the complexity of the text. We can ask lower-level, basic comprehension questions (DOK 1

Table 2.3. When to Apply Depth of Knowledge and Cognitive Rigor

Can be applied . . .	Should *not* be confused with . . .
• When evaluating how deeply students will engage with specific content • To interpret the intended complexity of standards, learning targets, instructional tasks, or test questions • When planning learning activities or assessment tasks and rubrics for all students, in any content areas, at any grade level • With strategic scaffolding to make a task or a text more accessible (e.g., chunking texts, collaborative discourse) without decreasing the complexity • To evaluate local curriculum expectations or to analyze results of assessment data and adjust instruction • As a reflective lens to foster teaching practices that support deeper learning	• A taxonomy, where students must master one level before moving on • More work, more effort, more steps to complete a task, or more difficult work • The value or importance of some tasks over others (all levels of DOK have value when used for an intended purpose) • Modifying a task for some students to change the difficulty • Verbs, a "verb wheel," or a specific set of prompts that indicate only one level of complexity • The complexity of the content or texts students are reading • Whether students complete tasks individually or with peers

or DOK 2) using a very complex text. We can ask lower-level basic comprehension questions using two texts (e.g., compare the settings in these stories). Questions like these would only be DOK 2, because the information needed to answer the question is most likely *stated explicitly* in the texts. Conversely, we can ask deeper, more rigorous questions using a wordless text. One of my favorite nonprint texts is the 2014 Caldecott Honor Book *Journey* (Becker, 2013a). Asking students to draw and support inferences using evidence from illustrations (or other nonprint texts) can be just as mentally challenging as reading and interpreting words in a print text (both are DOK 3).

If we were to ask students to read *Journey* and *Quest* (the second wordless text in this trilogy by Becker [2003b]) in order to examine aspects of author's craft across the texts, we set the stage for even greater mental challenges and higher cognitive demand (DOK 4).

> **Activity 2.4: Time to reflect: Post self-assessment**
>
> Now that you have read or discussed the common misconceptions and worked through the activities, return to the anticipation guide at the beginning of the module and complete step 3: Describe how your thinking has been clarified, validated, revised, or changed. Go to Appendix A, p. 89, to check your post-assessment responses.

SUMMING UP

Having tasks requiring multiple steps, asking students to read more texts, or using complex data or texts in routine ways doesn't usually lead to rigorous thinking. Deeper understanding is achieved when students dive into the concept, the scenario, the model, or the text(s) and come away with new understandings and insights, making connections that can transfer to future learning. Barbara Blackburn, author of numerous books about rigor, has written about the myths and misconceptions for as many years as I have. Table 2.3 summarizes both Barbara's and my thinking about how DOK and cognitive rigor can appropriately be applied.

> **Need a review of common misconceptions before completing the post-anticipation guide?** Watch an on-demand webinar, "Looking for Rigor in All the Right Places," at https://www.youtube.com/watch?v=gXFb5gdcogw from minute 4:30 to 25:10.

Deeper Instruction, Deeper Engagement, Deeper Learning

Key Questions Explored in Module 3:

- How are deep learning, learning transfer, and DOK connected?
- What is deep instruction and how can I use a cognitive rigor mindset to teach for transfer?
- Why, how, and when does a teacher's approach—or role—need to shift at each DOK level?

Over the years, the quest to understand "deep learning" has generated numerous research studies and various descriptions of the skills, knowledge, and dispositions students must possess to succeed in life after high school and in future careers. In *Education for Work and Life* (National Academies Press, 2012), the Committee on Defining Deeper Learning and 21st Century Skills states, "Young people need to develop a range of skills and knowledge that facilitate mastery and applications . . . in school subjects . . . and to develop skills, such as problem solving, critical thinking, communication, collaboration, and self-management—often referred to as '21st century skills'" (p. 1).

This range of skills, knowledge, and dispositions clearly requires both a better understanding of what deeper learning is and how educators can strategically employ strategies to support deep learning. Berger and colleagues (2016) stress the need for deep instruction that "honors the multidimensional nature of student achievement. . . . and not only prioritizes positive character and quality of work as essential components of student achievement, but also supports students to build mastery of knowledge and skills with more understanding and ownership" (p. 5).

We begin our discussion of deep learning with a widely accepted description from the Hewlett Foundation's *Deeper Learning Framework* (2013). My belief is that the six broad competencies outlined in this framework can only be actualized with deep instruction that leads to deeper student engagement and ultimately results in learning transfer.

The Six Broad Competencies for Deep Learning (Hewlett Foundation, 2013, pp. 2–5) are

- Mastering core academic content
- Thinking critically and solving complex problems
- Working collaboratively on complex tasks
- Communicating effectively
- Learning how to learn
- Developing an academic mindset

MAKING CONNECTIONS: SIX DEEPER LEARNING COMPETENCIES AND DOK

1. **Mastering core academic content** builds a foundation of procedural knowledge and conceptual understanding in each content discipline that students can draw from and transfer to new learning situations. DOK 1 and DOK 2 teaching strategies support students in mastering core content when they ask questions that focus students' attention; demonstrate/model how to use new tools or strategies; provide opportunities for students to practice routines, build schema, and make inferences; and strategically scaffold learning so that every student can access the concepts and skills to be learned (Hess, 2023).

2. **Thinking critically and solving complex problems** move beyond core content, requiring students to formulate questions to investigate, to use reasoning and analysis skills, and to explore problems and solutions from multiple perspectives. DOK 3 and DOK 4 teaching strategies support critical thinking when students in every content area, at every grade level, regularly practice solving nonroutine/novel problems. Teacher questioning strategies now shift to probing for reasoning, challenging logic chains, and extending student thinking to make connections with essential questions and the big ideas of each content discipline. (For an example of high-quality K–12 Critical Thinking rubrics, go to https://my.pblworks.org/resource/document/critical_thinking_rubrics.)
3. **Working collaboratively on complex tasks** builds both personal and workplace skills, when students learn to equitably consider multiple points of view, develop their own problem-solving steps to accomplish tasks, and monitor progress on shared group goals. At every DOK level, students can learn to give and receive feedback, set group goals, and work with peers to resolve differing points of view on how to solve problems or complete complex tasks. (For an example of high-quality K–12 Collaboration rubrics, go to https://www.best-future.org/resources/.)
4. **Communicating effectively** begins with learning how to use discipline-specific terminology, tools, and schemas to organize information in meaningful ways, give and receive feedback to clarify or elaborate on complex ideas or solutions, and demonstrate understanding by tailoring a message to the intended audience—including self, peers, adults, or the broader community (DOK 1–2). At DOK 3–4, communication moves beyond discipline-specific clarity and accuracy to "elaborated communication" (Hess, 2023; Hess & Gong, 2014), when students employ creative-productive thinking and a wider range of digital tools to access, organize, and deliver an engaging and coherent message (e.g., infographic, podcast, instructional video). (For an example of high-quality K–12 Communication rubrics, go to https://www.best-future.org/resources/.)
5. **Learning how to learn** requires shifting the traditional roles of teachers and students so that students take on increased agency and ownership in monitoring progress on personal goals for learning; seeking resources and help when needed; and reflecting on how strategies used, and decisions made, have impacted learning. A shift from DOK 1–2 to DOK 3–4 naturally requires teachers to give students more control of their learning (e.g., how they learn, how they demonstrate learning). Teachers now move from directing learning to strategically coaching learning. Metacognitive strategies—before, during, and after a lesson—guide students in learning how to organize their time, monitor their progress, and build confidence as they reflect on themselves as learners. (For an example of high-quality K–12 Self-Direction rubrics, go to https://www.best-future.org/resources/.)
6. **Developing an academic mindset** leads to positive attitudes and beliefs about oneself as a learner—influencing increased engagement with learning activities and a desire to actively learn from and with others. Academic mindsets build a strong sense of belonging within the learning community, where each student is willing to put forth effort, take risks, and persevere when confronted with productive struggle when completing complex tasks. At DOK 3–4, students are in more control of directing their learning, are actively involved in self-assessment and peer assessment, and are building greater confidence as learners. Strategies for using student-led assessments (e.g., conferencing, portfolio assessments) "support equitable assessment and grading practices. As we elevate each child's voice in class, we provide more opportunities to close the gap between *what we think* about their knowledge and skills and *what they know*" (Sackstein, 2024, p. 4).

Activity 3.1: Examining six deeper learning competencies

Review the descriptions of each of the deeper learning competencies. If you could place most of your focus on only five of them, which deeper learning competency would you place less time and effort on and why? (Hint: There isn't one correct answer, but every group of educators who have discussed this question with me have come to the same conclusion!)

Activity 3.2: What does deep instruction include?

As you read each research-based description of transfer and implications for deep instruction (in Table 3.1), identify key phrases that are relevant to your teaching.

Underlining means I do this consistently. **Add notes** describing your examples.

Circling means I want to learn more about how to do this. **Add your questions.**

LEARNING TRANSFER AND DEEP INSTRUCTION

For decades, educators and researchers have worked to explain learning processes and how educators can support learning transfer. "Transfer is the defining characteristic of deeper learning . . . Teaching for transfer begins with clear learning goals and valid ways to measure learning" (*Education for Work and Life*, National Academies Press, 2012, pp. 143–144). This research report goes on to say, "[I]t's worth noting that recent research on teaching and learning reveals that young children are capable of surprisingly sophisticated thinking and reasoning in science, mathematics, and other domains. . . . With careful guidance with carefully designed instruction, they can begin the process of deeper learning and development of transferable knowledge as early as preschool. . . . This process takes time and extensive practice over many years, suggesting that instruction for transfer should be introduced in the earliest grades and should be sustained throughout the K–12 years, as well as in post-secondary education" (pp. 162–165).

Table 3.1 illustrates an historical perspective of key ideas that have emerged about learning transfer, with implications for what deep instruction and teaching for transfer should include.

A closer review of the literature over the years (Biggs & Collis, 1982, 1989; Cree & Macauley, 2000; Doyle et al., 2006; Fisher et al., 2016; Hattie, 2023; Hess, 2018, 2023; Hess et al., 2020) also differentiates two types of transfer: replicating known routines the way they were taught (often called *near transfer*) and applying skills and knowledge in new/unfamiliar situations (called *far transfer*). Perkins and Salomon (1988) were among the first in the United States to discuss distinctions between near and far transfer. When students applied a skill or concept in a routine or typical way (e.g., decoding words in connected text, crafting a summary, completing math word problems, learning sports skills), they called it "low road" (near) transfer:

> Low road transfer reflects the automatic triggering of well-practiced routines in circumstances where there is a considerable similarity to the original context. High road transfer is not as dependent on superficial stimulus similarities, since through reflective abstraction, a person can often see through superficial differences to deeper analogies. (Perkins & Salomon, 1988, p. 29)

Examples of "high road" (far) transfer might include developing and conducting an investigation, analyzing perspectives and evidence in support of a claim, interpreting underlying themes, looking across datasets to determine why there may be differing interpretations, or applying skills in a game situation.

A SUPPORTIVE ENVIRONMENT FOR DEEP INSTRUCTION

Deep instruction does not happen by chance. Two critical requirements for deep instruction are (a)

Table 3.1. Learning Transfer and Deep Instruction

Evolving Descriptions of Learning Transfer	Implications for Deep Instruction
". . . the principle of learning, called *transfer,* describes a 2-part process: (1) the effect that past learning has on processing new learning; and (2) the degree to which the new learning will be useful to the learner in the future" (Sousa, 1995, p. 67).	Transfer depends on students accessing prior knowledge, seeing how it connects to new learning, and then applying the new learning in meaningful ways.
"To 'understand' has two general connotations . . . Transfer is when you take what you've learned in one way or context and use it in another, on your own. . . . An understanding is an idea that results from reflecting on and analyzing one's own learning: an important generalization, a new insight, a useful realization that makes sense out of prior experience . . ." (Wiggins & McTighe, 2011, p. 14, introducing transfer into their updated unit planning template 2.0).	Transfer becomes part of instructional planning—applying skills and knowledge in a new situation or when students are learning on their own. Self-reflection supports students' ability to make meaning of and extend what they learn and deepen understanding.
". . . *transfer of learning* is the ability to apply what you've learned in new settings . . . when you're asked to struggle with solving a problem before being shown how to solve it. The subsequent solution is better learned and more durably remembered" (Brown et al., 2014, pp. 85–86).	Transfer is applying skills and knowledge in a new situation. Experiencing productive struggle while working through a complex task (e.g., learning from mistakes) makes the learning more memorable.
In a study, learners either studied one example of how to solve a problem or were required to analyze two different kinds of problems to figure out the common elements. Researchers found that "learners who contrasted 2 problems were more likely to extract a general solution schema and transfer that schema to successfully solve new problems than were the learners who studied only one problem" (Brown et al., 2014, p. 278).	Exposure to multiple possible ways to solve problems is more effective in generalizing schemas to solve new, unfamiliar problems.
". . . defining how we learned, as well as what we learned, enables students to name the new skills they have gained in a lesson or unit that will be helpful to them again in the future" (Berger et al., 2016, p. 91).	Deep instruction includes metacognitive strategies, such as self-reflection, that enhance a student's ability to transfer learning to new situations.
"We sometimes treat learning like a switch that is turned on or off—either students learn something, or they don't. But learning is a spectrum, with surface learning and a lack of skill on one side and deep learning and mastery on the other. To better understand learning we need to know what happens in students' brains when they move from surface learning to deep learning" (Sriram, 2020, p. 2).	Challenging tasks increase the strength of brain signals. Repeated practice, guided by feedback; open-ended questions that require students to construct information; and creating productive struggle by giving students new/unfamiliar problems requiring application of prior learning strengthen brain capacity.
"The VL (Visible Learning) model involves a teacher who knows how to implement a range of teaching strategies to provide the student, when they seem *not* to understand, to give direction and redirection in terms of the content being understood and misunderstood, and thus, maximize the power of feedback received by the student. It is having the skill to get out of the way when learning is progressing towards the success criteria . . . and teaching students to become their own teachers" (Hattie, 2023, p. 7). "The performance of students with the most challenging goals are over 250% higher than the performance of subjects with the easiest goals" (Hattie, 2023, p. 314).	Hattie rank orders VL Influencers, indicating strategies that positively (or negatively) impact learning. (Note that an effect size of 0.40 = approximately one year's growth, indicating the potential to accelerate learning.) Below are effect sizes related to enhancing transfer and deep learning through deep instruction (Hattie, 2023, https://www.visiblelearningmetax.com/Influences): • (1.09) Teachers analyze tasks for cognitive complexity • (0.85) Teacher clarity to set appropriately challenging goals and provide support to all students • (0.86) Students' ability to transfer learning to new situations • (0.64) Self-efficacy/a student's concept of self as a learner; competence to attain the desired outcomes • (0.67) Self-directed learning

You can watch a short video of John Hattie explaining his research at https://www.visiblelearning.com

creating a supportive environment for thinking and learning and (b) shifting student roles from taking in and replicating information to produce knowledge that is relevant and applicable to real-world situations. John Hattie's research on the influence of classroom cohesion, the sense that students and teachers are working together toward positive learning gains (0.66), and teacher–student relationships (0.62) is compelling and often overlooked when planning rigorous instruction (Hattie, 2023, p. 202).

> **Activity 3.3: Watch (and reflect on) a TEDx Talk with Marc Chun**
>
> Watch "Diving into Deeper Learning," where Chun defines and provides examples of near-far transfer (16:30 min.) Access the video at https://www.youtube.com/watch?v=k6BmbdzPcrY.
>
> Then discuss: How can you apply the "007" versus "MacGyver" perspectives of transfer in your classroom?

Barbara Blackburn describes the classroom environment as basic to using any instructional strategies that increase rigor. "If you think of rigor as climbing a tower, the environment (for learning) is the strong foundation that allows students to climb to higher and higher levels" (2023, p. 153). Blackburn identifies several considerations that positively impact the learning environment: building positive relationships to better understand students' strengths and needs, attending to the verbal and nonverbal language that adults use to show respect and caring, organizing the physical environment to support deep instruction, and developing student ownership for learning by providing choices and decision-making about how learning will unfold and be shared.

A shift from surface learning to deep learning is only possible when students become actively immersed in challenging tasks, tasks requiring them to apply what they have learned and build upon that learning to construct new insights about the topic being explored and about themselves as learners. According to Hess,

> If we expect students to be curious and think deeply, we need to create a classroom culture where thinking is the norm. Do we value—and model—open-ended questions that have more than one answer? Do we value—and honor—learning from mistakes? Are we willing to shift some of our control to students so that they can begin to own—take responsibility for, reflect on, and value—their learning? (2023, p. 8)

Teachers must continually think about the intended purpose of each learning activity and how the design of questioning strategies and learning tasks will support students to be successful. If the purpose of a lesson is for students to acquire a foundation and build basic skills, then the teacher's role is to model and direct students in practicing those skills. However, if the purpose of the learning is for students to deepen and construct meaning for themselves, then the teacher's role needs to shift to that of a facilitator or strategic coach, allowing students to apply prior learning in an unfamiliar way and take more control of the learning processes or products. Recalling the mental processing required at each DOK level (see p. 16, Module 1) helps to determine whether students will be using near or far transfer. Will they be practicing skills the way they were taught (near transfer) or applying skills in novel situations (far transfer)? This requires teachers to balance past *practices that still work effectively and adopt new approaches intended to deepen learning.* Table 3.2 identifies general connections among DOK levels, learning intentions, and types of transfer.

COMPLEXITY MODELS DESIGNED TO ENCOMPASS BOTH NEAR AND FAR TRANSFER

In Module 1, some of the shortcomings of Bloom's taxonomy were discussed: Higher-order verbs do not necessarily lead to deep thinking, and lack of clarity to differentiate among taxonomy levels makes it difficult to discern whether the intended learning requires students to apply skills and concepts in a familiar situation or in a novel/nonroutine context. John Hattie, who has analyzed studies related to Bloom's taxonomy, states that

Table 3.2. Connecting DOK Levels and Learning Intentions to Types of Transfer

<table>
<tr><td>DOK 1
Acquire a Foundation</td><td>Students demonstrate knowledge and practice specific skills in isolation or in routine/familiar situations.</td><td rowspan="2">Near Transfer</td></tr>
<tr><td>DOK 2
Use, Connect, Conceptualize</td><td>Students apply skills and concepts in a generalized way, very much like the way they were originally taught, such as how to observe, summarize, explain, compare, predict, organize data, categorize, etc.</td></tr>
<tr><td>DOK 3
Deepen and Construct Meaning</td><td>Students apply prior knowledge and skills, delving deeply into open-ended questions that address problems, issues, or themes. They use inquiry and problem-solving to develop evidence to support, defend, or refute claims, solutions, or alternate approaches.</td><td rowspan="2">Far Transfer</td></tr>
<tr><td>DOK 4
Extend, Transfer, Broaden Meaning</td><td>Students generate new questions, in-depth insights, solutions, or applications that go beyond what was explicitly taught, such as investigating, triangulating evidence, uncovering competing perspectives, piloting and refining ideas, reflecting upon and revising for improved quality, etc.</td></tr>
</table>

> . . . there is little evidence supporting claims that these (levels of Bloom) increase cognitive complexity . . . as the levels mix ways of thinking with the processing required for completing tasks or answering questions, and there is surprisingly little evidence of its effect on improving lessons or impact on students. (Hattie, 2023, p. 51)

In other words, Bloom's taxonomy was not designed to differentiate near-far transfer.

It is worth noting that a taxonomy developed by John Biggs and Kevin Collis (1982) is the only taxonomy (that I've analyzed) that was intentionally designed to describe how learning progresses toward more sophisticated understanding and learning transfer. SOLO, which stands for Structure of the Observed Learning Outcome taxonomy, is currently used by educators across China, New Zealand, and Australia. SOLO describes four levels of complexity: uni-structural, multistructural, relational, and extended—abstract. Uni-structural responses and questions require the knowledge or use of only one piece of given information, fact, perspective, or idea obtained directly from the problem.

Multistructural responses are items requiring the use of two or more pieces of given information, facts, or ideas, each used separately (e.g., in two or more distinct steps, listing characteristics) with no integration of ideas. In contrast, "the two deep processes [relational and extended] . . . constitute a change of quality of thinking that is cognitively more challenging than surface ideas" (Hattie, 2023, pp. 51–52). "The relational level requires several aspects integrated so that the whole has a coherent structure and meaning. At the extended-abstract level the coherent whole is generalized to a higher level of extraction" (Hattie & Brown, 2004, p. 5).

The levels of SOLO are intended to provide a systematic way of describing how a learner's performance grows in complexity when mastering tasks. This general sequence of four levels can be used to guide teachers' development of specific learning targets and the assessment of specific outcomes based on observations of learning or can be used to develop personalized growth ladders students can use to monitor their own progress.

Table 3.3 briefly describes the four levels of SOLO, with my analysis comparing SOLO levels with DOK levels and the potential for learning that requires near versus far transfer. Because the SOLO levels are often shown with a series of simple visuals, I've created my own visuals to depict increasing understanding as connections and extensions are made. I think my visuals generally work for DOK and expand upon this idea in Module 4.

Considering the range of DOK level descriptors in the Hess Cognitive Rigor Matrices for each "verb" of Bloom's taxonomy, one conclusion that I quickly

Table 3.3. Comparing Levels of the SOLO Taxonomy with DOK Levels

SOLO Levels	Hess's visual interpretation of SOLO levels (expanding understanding)	SOLO descriptions: How well is something learned?	Verbs associated with each SOLO level (Biggs website)	Sample SOLO success criteria (Harte & Barrett, 2021)	Comparable DOK levels?	Near or Far transfer?
Uni-structural		Knows one thing/ one relevant aspect about a topic	Identify, name, follow simple procedure	I can share one idea.	1	Near transfer
Multistructural		Knows a few things/several relevant aspects about a topic, but doesn't connect them	Combine, describe, enumerate, perform, use serial skills, list	I can share many ideas.	1	Near transfer
Relational	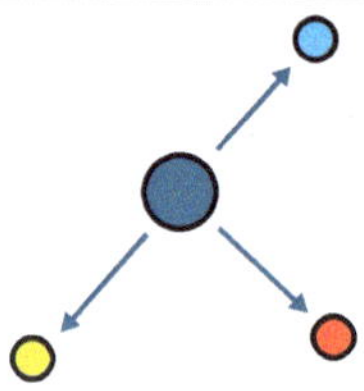	Able to connect ideas about a topic or integrate ideas into a structure or pattern	Analyze, apply, argue, compare-contrast, criticize, explain causes, relate, justify	I can connect and link my ideas.	2 or 3	Potential for Near or Far transfer
Extended—Abstract	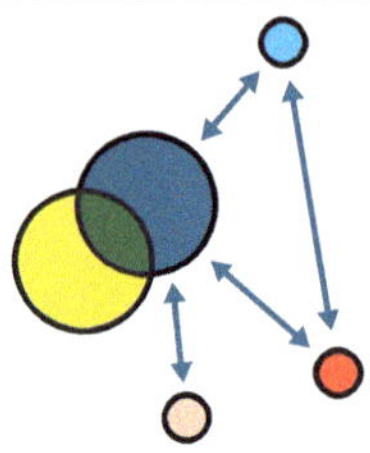	Can make connections beyond the original topic or domain	Create, formulate, generate, hypothesize, reflect, theorize, generalize to a new domain	I can link my ideas to other concepts.	3 or 4	Potential for Far transfer

came to was that, as with DOK levels, verbs alone were not useful in determining the complexity or depth of the learning students might be demonstrating at particular levels of SOLO. And, after reviewing multiple sources with examples of tasks, verbs, and success criteria associated with each SOLO level, I started to see different interpretations and varied examples, especially at the two upper levels of SOLO.

Below are three examples from Hattie and Brown (2004), aligned with the Relational level of SOLO, that made me question if they all required a similar level of cognitive processing or if any of them actually assessed deep learning or required far transfer. My current thinking is that more of the sample questions/tasks at the Relational level seem to be aligned with DOK 2, conceptual understanding.

- (Based on *Goldilocks*, p. 10) "Goldilocks eats the baby bear's food, breaks his chair, and sleeps in his bed. What does this tell us about the kind of person she is?"
- (Math, p. 13) "If 52 houses require 208 sticks, how many sticks do you need to be able to make 53 houses? (Answer 212)"
- (Science, p. 15) "Explain how distance from the sun and temperature are related."

The practice of moderation, commonly used throughout schools in Australia and New Zealand, could be useful in discerning tasks or student work samples at different SOLO (or DOK) levels.

> Moderation focuses on teachers working together to reach more in-depth understandings of their students'

> learning. . . . When moderation processes focus on learning, they support teachers in refining their understandings of what their students know and what they need to learn next. In this context, the moderation process should use fine-grained information about specific aspects of learning. (Heldsinger, 2021, p. 2)

My general conclusions? There are many similarities between the SOLO taxonomy and DOK in that they both strive to support an understanding of surface to deep learning, and both are useful in determining if students are making progress transferring learning in unfamiliar contexts (see Table 3.4). However, while the SOLO taxonomy can be used to analyze the range of complexity and sophistication of student responses to open-ended questions (e.g., "Why does it get dark at night?"), my focus and applications of DOK are on task design and intentional instructional planning. The clarity of being able to describe what teachers might be doing at each DOK level to elicit observable student thinking is stronger than I could find, especially with the two upper levels of SOLO. Not all tasks falling into the upper levels of SOLO seem to guarantee depth of learning above DOK 2 or DOK 3.

To learn more about the SOLO taxonomy, watch this webinar with Chris Harte and Tom Barrett (2021), "5 Ways to Power-up Your Teaching with The SOLO Taxonomy." You can access the webinar at https://www.youtube.com/watch?v=nStNc0ZCkH4

SHIFTING TEACHER–STUDENT ROLES AT EACH DOK LEVEL

At each DOK level, teachers are doing three key things *with intent*: (a) crafting questions to guide student thinking, (b) designing "actionable" tasks to actively engage learners and uncover what they do/do not understand, and (c) strategically scaffolding learning so that each learner can be successful (Hess, 2023). Guidance in designing actionable instruction and performance-based tasks that assess deeper learning (DOK 3–4) is elaborated on in Modules 5 and 6.

At DOK 1–2, students are acquiring a foundation, developing conceptual understanding, making connections, and applying skills and concepts in familiar tasks (e.g., word problems in math, comprehension questions in reading, developing hypotheses in science). At DOK 3, students are working on open-ended tasks—identifying relevant-irrelevant information or developing rationales after solving real-world math problems or analyzing design flaws in science and engineering investigations. Students are learning how to evaluate the quality and relevance of sources and developing evidence to support their reasoning. At DOK 4, students might be engaged in performance-based assessments—initiating an investigation or research study integrating information from multiple sources. They are also extending their understanding of what they are learning by making explicit connections to an essential question or a Big Idea of the content discipline.

Table 3.4. Comparing DOK With SOLO

Questions for Comparison	DOK	SOLO
Is it intended as a taxonomy?	No	Yes
How many levels are there?	4	4
Are verb lists associated with each level useful in analyzing surface versus deeper learning?	No	No
Was it designed to clearly differentiate surface-level learning from deep learning?	Yes	Yes
Is it intended for designing learning and assessment tasks requiring different levels of cognitive engagement?	Yes	Yes
Is it intended to be used to evaluate student responses, regardless of the actual task or question?	No	Yes
Can tools be aligned with levels to help students monitor their own progress toward deep learning?	Yes	Yes
Can tools be aligned with levels to help teachers design learning for near-far transfer?	Yes	Yes

Table 3.5. Shifting Roles: Moving From Teacher-Directed to Student-Driven Learning

DOK Levels	Teacher Roles	Student Roles
1 Acquire a Foundation	Asks questions to focus attention *(Who? What? Where? How? When?)* Directs, leads, demonstrates, defines, provides guided practice Scaffolds for content access and focus	Acquires vocabulary, facts, rules Memorizes, recites, quotes, restates Retrieves information using tools, resources Practices and self-monitors routine skills Clarifies procedures, asks for support in using resources, tools
2 Use, Connect, & Conceptualize	Asks questions to build schema: differentiate parts-whole, classify, draw out inferences *(Why does this work? Under what conditions?)* Models/thinks aloud to uncover relationships Scaffolds to build conceptual understanding Provides examples/non-examples	Explains relationships, sorts, classifies, compares, organizes information Makes predictions based on estimates, observations, prior knowledge Proposes problems or issues/questions to be investigated Raises conceptual or strategy-based questions Selects and uses tools for specific purpose
3 Deepen & Construct Meaning	Asks questions to probe reasoning and promote peer discourse/self-reflection Links lessons to Big Ideas *(Where else would this apply? What concepts/principles could be used to solve this?)* Designs tasks requiring proof, justification, and analysis of evidence quality and accuracy Scaffolds how to develop and investigate a range of questions	Uncovers relevant, accurate, credible information, flaws in a design, or proposed solution and links with "Big Ideas" Plans how to develop supporting (hard) evidence for conclusions or claims Researches, tests, refines ideas, solves non-routine problems; perseveres Self-assesses; uses feedback to improve performance; sets goals; monitors progress
4 Extend, Transfer, & Broaden Meaning	Asks Essential/Driving Questions to extend thinking, explore sources, broaden perspectives *(Are there potential biases? Can you propose an alternative model?)* Scaffolds use of relevant, valid resources, peer-to-peer discourse; self-reflection, links to Big Ideas	Initiates, transfers, and *constructs* new knowledge/insights linked to "Big Ideas" Modifies, creates, elaborates based on analysis and interpretation of information from multiple sources Investigates real-world problems and issues; perseveres; manages time-task Generates self-assessment; uses feedback to improve performance Sets goals, manages time, evaluates progress

Source: Hess (2013). Used with permission.

College- and career-readiness literature promotes the importance of deep learning and developing metacognitive skills, student agency, and an academic mindset (Berger et al., 2016; Hattie, 2023; Hess & Gong, 2014; Hess et al., 2025; Hewlett Foundation, 2013; National Academies Press, 2012; Sackstein, 2024; VanderArk, 2017; Wiliam et al., 2024). Shifting teacher–student roles is one concrete way classroom teachers can begin to plan for and nurture student agency and personalized learning. This was one of my six epiphanies about applying DOK and cognitive rigor:

> [W]hen we design with rigor and deeper learning in mind, DOK levels become a subtle but powerful force

> in shifting from teacher-directed to student-driven learning. I believe that this is the single most important use of DOK—to guide the design of rigorous, student-directed learning. (Hess, 2023, p. 23)

Table 3.5 illustrates the subtle shifts of teacher—student roles at each DOK level, describing observable shifts in teacher questioning strategies, task design, and scaffolding to support learning and the related observable student behaviors.

Activity 3.4: Time to reflect

When have you acquired skills and knowledge that you later transferred to complete a more complex, real-world task (e.g., in sports, work-based, hobby/interest-related)?

- How did your teachers or mentors support that learning? (See teacher roles above.)
- How did your role as a learner shift as you moved from being a novice to more of an emerging expert? (See student roles above.)

SUMMING UP

Most educators would agree that teachers take on different roles when planning and delivering instruction. Directed teaching is when explicit instruction and modeling are used to help learners acquire new information and basic skills. At times, teachers will shift to become facilitators, guiding learners to actively process information or to practice how to use a new procedure. When teachers act as directors and facilitators, students receive and reproduce what has been presented (DOK 1) and develop basic conceptual understanding (DOK 2). However, these teacher roles are not effective when we want students to engage in self-direction, collaboration, creative problem-solving, and reasoning activities. College- and career-readiness goals establish expectations for all students to demonstrate learning through the acquisition of content knowledge and skills *and* to have the ability to transfer that learning to new and more complex tasks over time. Planning lessons that ask students to respond to open-ended questions requiring supporting evidence, solving problem-based performance tasks, or reflecting on their own learning requires teachers to shift from directing to coaching students and encouraging them to drive some of the learning, a prime motivation for deep learning. Deep learning occurs when students are motivated to exert the effort to learn.

> Students learn more deeply when they attribute their performance to effort rather than to their ability . . . when they have the goal of mastering the material rather than the goal of performing well or not performing poorly . . . when they expect to succeed on a learning task and value the learning task . . . when they have the belief that they are capable of achieving the task at hand . . . when they believe that intelligence is changeable rather than fixed . . . and when they are interested in the learning task. (National Research Council, 2000 pp. 164–165)

Applying a Cognitive Rigor Mindset to Standards, Competencies, and Curriculum

Key Questions Explored in Module 4:

- How do we use the Hess CRMs to accurately interpret our standards or competencies with regard to task complexity or performance expectations?
- How are cognitive rigor, standards/competencies, and success criteria related?
- How can curriculum design articulate the path to deeper learning for students and the transfer goals they are working toward?

Standards are long-term learning goals describing what students should know and be able to do by the end of each school year. According to Hess, in Hougen and Smartt (2020),

> The responsibility for establishing standards has evolved since the time of the one-room schoolhouse when it was the teacher who decided what students would learn each year. This often resulted in different teachers setting different standards for different students. The lack of consistency in setting high expectations for all students led to inequities—with some students making progress and other students leaving school not knowing how to read or write proficiently. (p. 42)

Over time, individual states and national organizations (e.g., National Coalition for Core Arts Standards [NCCAS]; Society of Health and Physical Educators [SHAPE America]; National Council for the Social Studies) developed standards for students in each grade level or grade span for each content area. However, many of the inequities and challenges in meeting the individual needs of students continued, and standards implementation often varied greatly from one state to another.

The push for college and career readiness (CCR) has led to the adoption of standards that now look more similar than different state to state and emphasize the need to provide learning opportunities so that *all students* can achieve the same high academic learning goals by the time they graduate from high school. Instructional approaches such as the Multi-Tiered System of Supports (MTSS) framework, social-emotional learning (SEL), differentiation, and allowing for dual enrollment in college courses while still in high school have arisen out of the need to meet all students "where they are" in their learning process in order to move each student's learning forward.

In addition to content standards, many school districts and states have adopted a competency-based learning (CBL) approach, setting broader academic and personal learning goals for all K–12 students than academic standards do. Competencies are often described in a districtwide document called a portrait (or profile) of the graduate (POG) or portrait of a learner (POL). For example, a POG might include a broadly stated competency in effective communication skills that applies skills and concepts drawn from multiple reading, writing, listening, speaking, and digital learning standards.

In this module, we will use the Hess matrices to examine the connection between the content to be learned in standards or competencies and the cognitive rigor applied to standards-based and competency-based learning, and how curriculum planning—specifically a storyboarding approach—can convey how the standards and competencies to be learned move toward a deeper level of student understanding.

This module addresses developing an understanding of how content (standards/competencies) and DOK are related helps to establish performance expectations, which is useful when planning curriculum and instruction and designing assessments.

USING THE HESS MATRICES TO INTERPRET THE RIGOR OF A STANDARD

Using standards to guide the planning of instruction and assessment begins with an intentional process to determine what learning is implied by the standards and establishing agreed-upon expectations for how students will demonstrate that learning. Teacher clarity about the intent of standards is especially important when using standards-based grading and reporting, because assessments used in grading are only valid when test questions match what is described in the standards and learning expectations.

Interpreting the learning intended by a content standard (sometimes referred to as "unwrapping" standards) requires an understanding of several related concepts: cognitive rigor, depth of knowledge (DOK), and the difference between a content standard and a performance expectation. The first step in unwrapping standards involves analyzing *what* content (skills and concepts) students will learn, and then determining *how/how deeply* students will engage with the content. This is not simply about looking at verbs (e.g., solve, write), but about further interpreting actions students will apply to solve (e.g., write a number sentence, add, use a representation) or write (e.g., organize ideas, use transitions, cite evidence). This initial unwrapping process helps teachers to decide which learning activities can best meet the expectations articulated in the standards at a given grade level and how to develop success criteria that articulate that learning in student-friendly language. "Success criteria provide the parameters that establish what success looks like for the learning intentions of that day" (Almarode et al., 2021, p. 2).

> **Watch a very short video showing how an elementary teacher adds clarity to success criteria by setting parameters for writing a good "how-to" book**. With teacher clarity, there are no secrets! Students know what's expected of them. Access the video at https://www.youtube.com//watch?v=8S3MuldH14s.

Over the past 2 decades, my friend Larry Ainsworth has developed and refined a succinct process for unwrapping standards using the Hess CRMs to develop greater teacher clarity when designing lessons, units of study, and assessments. Why is teacher clarity so important in this process? Numerous research studies indicate that "teacher clarity leads to alignment of goals, learning strategies, success criteria, and feedback" (Hattie, 2023, p. 307). Simply put, planning and teaching with clarity has a significant impact on advancing student learning. "Educators unwrap essential standards to receive the gift of greater clarity" (Ainsworth, 2024, p. 3).

Figure 4.1. Plotting Hattie's Visual Learning Influencers Along an "Effectiveness" Scale

John Hattie Rank Orders Visual Learning Influencers Along a Scale.
Practices Related to Approximately One Year of Learning = 0.40 (Hattie, 2023).

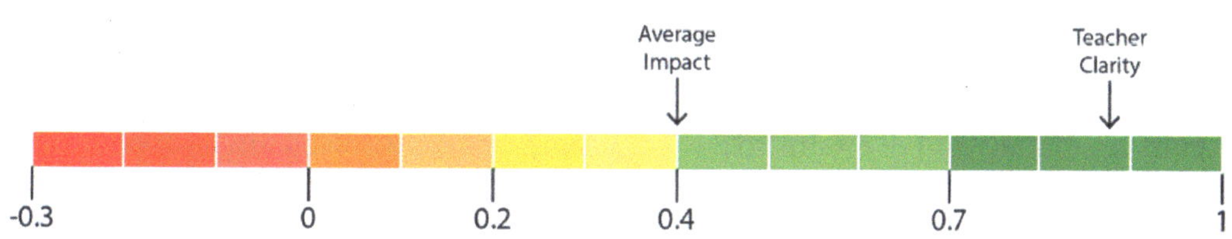

Source: Adapted from Ainsworth (2024, p. 3). Used with permission.

Ainsworth stresses the importance of teacher clarity—which has an impressive Hattie VLI effect size of 0.85 (Hattie, 2023, p. 217), illustrated in Figure 4.1. When determining how to design units of study aligned with standards (or competencies, which we will discuss later in the module), teacher clarity is essential.

In his work over the years with schools, Ainsworth has found that using Bloom's taxonomy or DOK levels alone for analyzing standards is not as effective at using the content-specific Hess matrices. The Hess CRMs have multiple entry points (Bloom and DOK) for both unwrapping the standards and developing a series of success criteria.

Ainsworth's unwrapping process begins with analyzing content standards to determine the concepts and skills to be learned. Using the Hess CRMs for the related content area, teachers are guided to first identify the level of Bloom's taxonomy listed along the left side of the Hess Matrix. For example, I've color-coded the **content/concepts** to be learned and **skills to be applied** in the following middle school science standard: Students will **develop and use a model to describe** the **function of a cell as a whole** and the **ways parts of cells contribute to the function**. Figure 4.2 uses yellow highlighting to illustrate how the Hess CRM for Math-Science can be used to identify the intended rigor of the learning described in this science standard.

- Step 1: Using descriptions of the levels of Bloom's revised taxonomy in the far-left column of the Hess CRM for math-science, we can identify that students will be carrying out a procedure (Bloom's Level 3, Apply) and breaking content into constituent parts (Bloom's level 4, Analyze). These two levels of Bloom are highlighted (in Figure 4.2) and recorded in a graphic organizer.
- Step 2: Using descriptions of DOK levels 1, 2, 3, and 4 in the four corresponding columns, we again look for descriptions of how students are expected to demonstrate learning: using models and diagrams to represent or explain science concepts (intersects with Bloom's Understand level) and constructing a model when given criteria (intersects with Bloom's Analyze level). Both of these are listed under DOK 2. These are also highlighted (Figure 4.2) and recorded in a graphic organizer.

This quick analysis using the Hess Math-Science CRM tells teachers that the focus of this standard is on conceptual understanding, so performance expectations would primarily be written as a series of success criteria at DOK 1 and DOK 2 levels. This does not prevent a teacher from adding a performance task (DOK 3) to the unit of study when students are learning about cell structures and functions. A DOK 3 performance-based assessment would ask students to transfer and solidify earlier learning about cells. According to Ainsworth,

> Zeroing in on what each "unwrapped" concept-skill is calling for in terms of rigor is a valuable aid in planning the sequence of instruction, classroom learning tasks, and formative and summative assessments so that teachers can directly align the levels of rigor . . . within each unit of study . . . a continuing reminder to raise the level of their daily instruction to correspond with the rigor of the unwrapped essential standards. (2024, pp. 14–15)

Table 4.1 illustrates how teachers might use the initial unwrapping information to develop performance expectations for content standards within a unit of study. We can align DOK levels with performance expectations because they describe how students will interact with the content (concepts and skills) to demonstrate learning in a variety of situations. Note that a range of DOK levels is possible when describing performance expectations for a standard if we consider what students will be doing to acquire foundational skills, develop conceptual understanding, and then deepen and transfer that learning.

Performance expectations describe *how* and *how deeply* students will engage with the content and apply their knowledge to demonstrate what they have learned. This distinction is important because the same content (e.g., informational writing; operations with decimals) might appear at different grade levels, with different performance expectations. And there can be more than one performance expectation (DOK levels) for the same content standard at a given grade level.

Figure 4.2. Analyzing the Intent of a Science Standard Using the Hess CRM

TOOL 2

HESS COGNITIVE RIGOR MATRIX | MATH-SCIENCE CRM

Integrating Depth-of-Knowledge Levels with Bloom's Cognitive Process Dimensions

Revised Bloom's Taxonomy	DOK Level 1 Recall and Reproduction	DOK Level 2 Skills and Concepts	DOK Level 3 Strategic Thinking or Reasoning	DOK Level 4 Extended Thinking
Remember Retrieve knowledge from long-term memory, recognize, recall, locate, identify	o Recall, observe, and recognize facts, principles, properties o Recall/ identify conversions among representations or numbers (e.g., customary and metric measures)			
Understand Construct meaning, clarify, paraphrase, represent, translate, illustrate, give examples, classify, categorize, summarize, generalize, infer a logical conclusion, predict, compare–contrast, match like ideas, explain, construct models	o Evaluate an expression o Locate points on a grid or number on number line o Solve a one-step problem o Represent math relationships in words, pictures, or symbols o Read, write, compare decimals in scientific notation	o Specify and explain relationships (e.g., non examples or examples; cause-effect) o Make and record observations o Explain steps followed o Summarize results or concepts o Make basic inferences or logical predictions from data or observations o Use models or diagrams to represent or explain mathematical concepts o Make and explain estimates	o Use concepts to solve non routine problems o Explain, generalize, or connect ideas using supporting evidence o Make and justify conjectures o Explain thinking or reasoning when more than one solution or approach is possible o Explain phenomena in terms of concepts	o Relate mathematical or scientific concepts to other content areas, other domains, or other concepts o Develop generalizations of the results obtained and the strategies used (from investigation or readings) and apply them to new problem situations
Apply Carry out or use a procedure in a given si tuation; carry out (apply to a familiar task), or use (apply) to an unfamiliar task	o Follow simple procedures (recipe-type directions) o Calculate, measure, apply a rule (e.g., rounding) o Apply algorithm or formula (e.g., area, perimeter) o Solve linear equations o Make conversions among representations or numbers, or within and between customary and metric measures	o Select a procedure according to criteria and perform it o Solve routine problem applying multiple concepts or decision points o Retrieve information from a table, graph, or figure and use it solve a problem requiring multiple steps o Translate between tables, graphs, words, and symbolic notations (e.g., graph data from a table) o Construct models given criteria	o Design investigation for a specific purpose or research question o Conduct a designed investigation o Use concepts to solve non routine problems o Use and show reasoning, planning, and evidence o Translate between problem and symbolic notation when not a direct translation	o Select or devise approach among many alternatives to solve a problem o Conduct a project that specifies a problem, identifies solution paths, solves the problem, and reports results
Analyze Break into constituent parts, determine how parts relate, differentiate between relevant-irrelevant, distinguish, focus, select, organize, outline, find coherence, deconstruct	o Retrieve information from a table or graph to answer a question o Identify whether specific information is contained in graphic representations (e.g., table, graph, T-chart, diagram) o Identify a pattern or trend	o Categorize, classify materials, data, figures based on characteristics o Organize or order data o Compare-contrast figures or data o Select appropriate graph and organize and display data o Interpret data from a simple graph o Extend a pattern	o Compare information within or across data sets or texts o Analyze and draw conclusions from data, citing evidence o Generalize a pattern o Interpret data from complex graph o Analyze similarities–differences between procedures or solutions	o Analyze multiple sources of evidence o Analyze complex or abstract themes o Gather, analyze, and evaluate information
Evaluate Make judgments based on criteria, check, detect inconsistencies or fallacies, judge, critique	"UG"—unsubstantiated generalizations = stating an opinion without providing any support for it!		o Cite evidence and develop a logical argument for concepts or solutions o Describe, compare, and contrast solution methods o Verify reasonableness of results	o Gather, analyze, and evaluate information to draw conclusions o Apply understanding in a novel way, provide argument or justification for the application
Create Reorganize elements into new patterns or structures, generate, hypothesize, design, plan, produce	o Brainstorm ideas, concepts, or perspectives related to a topic	o Generate conjectures or hypotheses based on observations or prior knowledge and experience	o Synthesize information within one data set, source, or text o Formulate an original problem given a situation o Develop a scientific/mathematical model for a complex situation	o Synthesize information across multiple sources or texts o Design a mathematical model to inform and solve a practical or abstract situation

Table 4.1. Developing Performance Expectations for Content Standards

Grade Level	Content Area	Sample Content Standard	Learning Intended in Content Standard: What skills and concepts will students acquire and understand?	Performance Expectations: How (and how deeply) will students engage and apply their knowledge (with DOK levels)?
1	Math	Solve word problems that call for addition of three whole numbers whose sum is less than or equal to 20 (using objects, drawings, equations with a symbol for the unknown).	• Understand the terms: sum, addition, equal, symbol, unknown. • Add 1, 2, and 3 whole numbers. • Write number sentences. • Solve number sentences using manipulatives, drawings, symbols. • Create story problems solved by adding.	Perform routine operation—addition of whole numbers (DOK 1). • Interpret and represent addition problems with drawings, objects, equations, or symbols (DOK 2). • Perform routine operations within a word problem (DOK 2). • Transfer goal: Solve open-ended problems using addition strategies and reasoning (DOK 3).
3	Reading Informational Texts	Compare and contrast the most important points and key details presented in two texts on the same topic.	• Know structure of informational texts: topic, introduction, key ideas, supporting details for each idea, conclusions. • Use of informational texts features (e.g., subheading, bold print, diagrams) and the information they provide in support of key ideas. • Locate details to support interpretations of print/nonprint texts.	• Summarize key ideas in one text (DOK 2). • Locate and use details (text evidence) to compare similarities and differences (DOK 2). • Develop an explanation about differing perspectives on a topic, from two sources, using supporting evidence (DOK 4).
4	Writing	Conduct short research projects that build knowledge through investigation of different aspects of a topic.	• Know structure of informational texts: topic, introduction, key ideas, supporting details for each idea, conclusions. • Use of informational texts features to organize information (e.g., subheading, bold print, diagrams) and provide support of key ideas. • Distinguish relevant and irrelevant facts. • Distinguish facts and opinions. • Write a variety of complete sentences. • Apply grammar usage and mechanics when composing paragraphs.	• Generate questions a report might answer (DOK 1, DOK 2). • Summarize key ideas from one text (DOK 2). • Organize information from more than one source to illustrate how key concepts and relevant issues are connected (DOK 3). • Apply strategies for text cohesion, transition, and organization of ideas in a multiparagraph composition (DOK 2, DOK 3). • Develop a logical progression of ideas, with supporting evidence from more than one source (DOK 4). • Express ideas coherently (using grammar, punctuation, precise language, etc.) (DOK 1 or 2).
5	Reading Literature	Determine a theme of a story, drama, or poem from details in the	• Apply structures and literary elements of different genre of literary texts (story, drama, poem).	• Summarize key events in a literary text, including how problems are solved (DOK 2).

Table 4.1. (*continued*)

Grade Level	Content Area	Sample Content Standard	Learning Intended in Content Standard: What skills and concepts will students acquire and understand?	Performance Expectations: How (and how deeply) will students engage and apply their knowledge (with DOK levels)?
		text, including how characters respond to challenges or how the speaker in a poem reflects upon a topic; summarize the text.	• Distinguish between theme(s) implied in literary texts versus a summary of what the text says explicitly. • Track plots/storylines in literary texts unfold as characters take on and resolve challenges.	• Use details (text evidence) to describe how characters respond to and resolve challenges (DOK 1 or 2). • Use and explain how details (text evidence) support interpretation of theme(s) (DOK 3). • Transfer goal: Analyze two texts with similar themes (DOK 4).
6–8	Science	**Develop and use a model to describe** the **function of a cell as a whole** and the **ways parts of cells contribute to the function.**	• Describe the **function of a cell as a whole.** • Describe the **ways parts of cells contribute to the function.** • **Use a model to describe relationships of parts and whole.** • **Develop a model.**	• Define content-specific terms (DOK 1). • Retrieve information (from a diagram or model) in order to answer questions (DOK 1). • Specify and explain relationships (DOK 2). • Use models to represent relationships (DOK 2). • Construct a model using given criteria (DOK 2). • Transfer goal: Conduct an investigation examining cell functions (DOK 3).
Your grade level	Your content area	Your standard		

Stories From the Field

When working with a district at the beginning of the school year, we took time to help teachers deconstruct standards based on their state assessment data. To do this, we looked not only at the standard but also at the testing resources connected to the state assessment (test specifications, blueprints, released testing items, performance level descriptors, etc.). Using a template, the teams broke down standards that showed where students scored poorly.

The template consisted of the following questions: What do students need to know and be able to do? Identify the skills/concepts. Identify the DOK levels within the standard. What is the academic vocabulary in the standard? What resources, instructional strategies, and assessments will be used?

Through this collaborative review of the data examining rigor of standards, we found that there was one common ELA standard throughout the majority of grade levels where performance was consistently weak.

Comments from staff included: "I learned that I should use the results from the student performance scores to evaluate which standard is used more often on a state test and to review which standards are most difficult for students to grasp. . . . Unpacking the standards is a practice I should use more often in my professional world. It pushes me to study the content and intended rigor in my weekly units, too." —Karen Boch, educational consultant

Activity 4.1: Time to apply—Unwrap a content standard and develop performance expectations

Study Table 4.1. Complete the table by adding a content standard for your grade level. Using the Hess CRM for your content area (found in Appendix B), unwrap the content standard and list *what* students need to learn. Then develop performance expectations using one or more DOK levels describing *how (and how deeply)* students will engage with the content.

On most state assessments, performance expectations are called "performance level descriptors" and are written to encompass multiple content standards rather than each individual standard. For example, a performance expectation in reading might be stated as

Students will read and understand increasingly complex print and nonprint literary texts, and provide text details to support comprehension, interpretations, and analyses.

This example is based on students mastering several content standards in reading—from basic comprehension to deeper analyses of texts. An assessment for this performance standard would include a combination of test questions at different DOK levels—asking students to describe, interpret, and analyze parts of texts using literary text passages.

DEVELOPING SUCCESS CRITERIA APPLYING DOK-LEVEL DESCRIPTORS

A major aspect of teacher clarity consists of learning intentions and success criteria—the research evidence cannot be overstated. In 2023, Hattie updated the overall effect size of success criteria to be 0.64 (p. 309). Fisher et al. (2020) states,

> Careful analysis of content standards benefits those who need to teach them—the educators themselves. Through the process of discussion and debate, colleagues identify what students should know and be able to do, and thus prevent the inevitable "creep" that occurs when textbooks and activities, not the standards, begin to drive instruction. . . . when discussions at a grade-level meeting are focused more on covering a chapter in a textbook rather than the learning outcomes, it is a telltale sign that the standard has been lost. (p. xvi)

The best way to increase teacher clarity is to use a collaborative process, such as within the structure of a professional learning community/PLC (e.g., grade-level or cross-grade content teams). Success criteria should be written in the first person, speaking as the student would speak. For example:

- I can locate details to answer a question (DOK 1).
- I can describe the relationship between rational and irrational numbers (DOK 2).
- I can design *or* conduct an investigation to determine the effects of the net force acting on an object (DOK 3).
- I can design *and* conduct an *original* investigation to analyze the influence of culture and place on music and art produced in the 1950s (DOK 4).

Notice that success criteria can address learning at any DOK level. Within a unit of study, there will be multiple DOK levels represented as students move from being novice learners who are acquiring a foundation of concepts and skills to being expert learners who can transfer their learning and teach those skills to others.

After unwrapping a standard, brainstorm a list of possible success criteria with your colleagues and then review them to identify which ones would be the most appropriate in terms of clarity, specificity, kid-friendliness, and alignment with the standard(s) being taught. After multiple success criteria have been developed for a unit of study, teachers can determine an instructional sequence that moves learners from "just getting started" to "I got this!"

Table 4.2 combines two key ideas that support development of success criteria: the intended

Table 4.2. DOK Levels, Observable Success Criteria (Engagement), and Content/Skills to Be Learned

DOK Level + Purpose	Hess's DOK Visual Expanding Knowledge	Success Criteria from Novice to Expert I/we can . . .	Applying Standards or Academic or Personal Competencies
1 **Acquire Foundation** Near Transfer		• Follow specific steps to complete routine tasks • Retrieve/locate/recall facts, details, terms • Use required tools/resources for specific purpose • Practice and self-monitor routine skills/processes • Perform routine operations; apply rules • Recite/paraphrase definitions, principles	Practicing skills and knowledge in isolation, with guidance: I can . . . I can . . . I can . . .
2 **Use, Connect, Conceptualize** Near Transfer	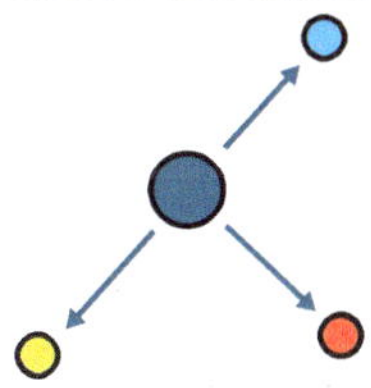	• Explain relationships (cause-effect; compare-contrast; if-then) • Organize or graph information • Summarize, sequence, sort, classify, infer • Predict based on observations, prior knowledge • Pose conceptual questions, problems, or topics to investigate • Select and use tool/strategy for a specific purpose (e.g., word problem, collect data)	Building conceptual connections, practicing routine tasks: I can . . . I can . . . I can . . .
3 **Deepen and Construct Meaning** Far Transfer	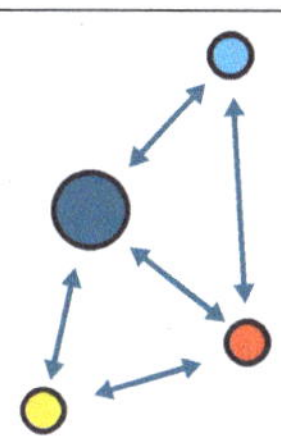	• Uncover relevant, accurate, credible information, flaws in a design/claims • Investigate questions that explore underlying/implied meanings • Use criteria to evaluate or develop supporting evidence for conclusions, solutions, claims, point of view/POV. • Conduct/revise/refine investigations • Solve non-routine problems • Self-assess/reflect; use feedback to improve quality • Make connection to Big Ideas or themes	Deepening knowledge and skills tackling complex, open-ended tasks: I can . . . I can . . . I can . . .
4 **Extend Transfer Broaden Meaning** Far Transfer	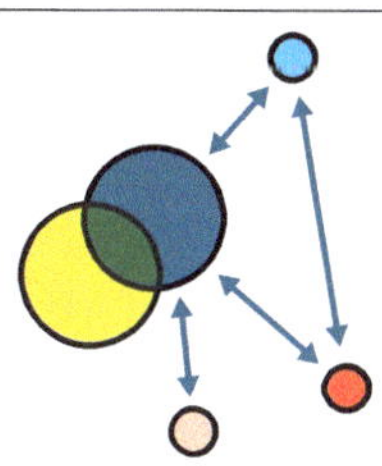	• Initiate, transfer, and construct new knowledge • Modify, create, elaborate, or evaluate based on analysis or integration of information from multiple sources • Raise novel questions, investigate multi-faceted real-world problems or issues • Self-assess/reflect; use feedback to improve quality • *Develop broader* insights linked to Big Ideas, Essential Questions, or themes	Transferring and expanding knowledge and skills using multiple sources, open-ended challenges, and self-directed learning: I can . . . I can . . . I can . . .

purpose for learning at each DOK level and observable, measurable activities that students might be engaged with in a given content area.

First, a brief explanation about reading this table. In Module 3, I compared characteristics of DOK with the SOLO taxonomy (Table 3.3) and created visuals to illustrate each of the SOLO levels. The levels of SOLO are not the same as the four DOK levels, but the similarities between the two models inspired me to create visuals to describe each DOK level (in Table 4.2). At DOK 1, we start with multiple (random) dots, representing pieces of information that have not yet been connected in meaningful ways. At this level, the pieces of information might represent a list of details or definitions. At DOK 1, students might memorize and follow steps in a process, but they are not able to explain how or why the steps connect. At DOK 2, the blue dot starts to become larger because connections are being made between this piece of information and other pieces of information. Perhaps the student is making inferences about data collected, making predictions based on observations, or classifying information using criteria (e.g., sorting geometric shapes by the number of sides). Note that the "connection arrows" only go in one direction—from the source question to supporting ideas. At DOK 3, the blue dot becomes even larger, representing expanding understanding due to multiple connections (double-sided arrows) being made within and across other pieces of information. At DOK 3, students are connecting strategies they've learned to solve open-ended problems, or they are applying knowledge of author's craft as they analyze a text in multiple ways. The focus at DOK 3 is deepening and constructing knowledge while examining one text, one investigation, one concept, or one problem-solving activity. At DOK 4, not only does the blue dot expand, but it expands in relation to other chunks of information—the yellow dot has also become larger and the intersection of yellow and blue becomes green, representing new insights and perhaps connections to bigger ideas and essential questions of the discipline. Connections across pieces of information become supporting information for transferring learning and broadening meaning.

Activity 4.2: Time to apply—Developing success criteria at different DOK levels

After unwrapping a content standard, use your performance expectations to develop increasingly complex success criteria for a unit of study. Fill in the far-right column of the table, applying your content with "I can" statements similar to the sample DOK-level stems in Table 4.2. Don't worry if a single standard doesn't "reach" DOK 4. Most units of study integrate multiple standards. That's how you get to DOK 4 and far learning transfer!

Stories From the Field

In Utah, we have tried to position cognitive rigor at the center of our statewide efforts. Our portrait of a graduate (POG) identifies the knowledge, skills, and dispositions that our communities are seeking to build in their students, and the only way to build skills and dispositions is through cognitively rigorous experiences. We have developed a personalized, competency-based learning (PCBL) framework to help communities support their students in reaching the POG. The five components of this framework are basically all geared toward helping communities provide cognitively rigorous experiences for their students. The framework includes creating a culture of learning present throughout a school focused on teacher clarity, high expectations for all students, and strong relationships. It also includes student agency, focused around ensuring students are consistently metacognitive about their own learning and that they have voice and choice in how to demonstrate what they know.

Because competency-based assessment systems are strongly correlated with cognitively rigorous tasks, we included this in our framework, as well as customized supports to ensure that those students who need more support to demonstrate competency have it and those who demonstrate it quickly can extend their learning, ensuring all students are engaged in cognitively rigorous experiences. The final component in our PCBL framework is social-emotional learning, which prepares students to manage their relationships, collaborations, and potential hardships that they come across while learning. —Nathan Auck, Utah State Board of Education

Table 4.3. Comparing Standards and Competencies

Standards	Competencies
• Written in teacher language (using educational terminology) • Variable grain sizes, some encompassing broad ideas and others describing discrete skills • Many in each grade level and content area, making them less manageable to track individually • Competency or proficiency on one standard does not mean that students can apply those skills or concepts in a variety of more complex tasks • Varied applications across courses • Post-assessments may not indicate competence/proficiency or time for a student to move on • DOK levels vary, with most standards written only at DOK levels 1 or 2 • Usually, must be combined with other standards in rich performance-based tasks to assess deeper thinking and transfer (DOK levels 3 or 4)	• Written in student-friendly language (*I can*) • Larger grain size, encompassing multiple standards (skills, procedures, concepts, and application) in more complex tasks • Fewer overall in each grade level or content area, making them more manageable to track student progress and reinforce • Lend themselves to comparable applications across courses and learning opportunities • Assessments are used to determine whether students are ready to advance or need additional support • Describe deeper learning (DOK levels 3 and 4), including transfer of skills and concepts and creation of knowledge • May describe academic or personalized skills and concepts

Source: Hess et al., 2020, p. 68. Used with permission.

MOVING FROM STANDARDS-BASED TO COMPETENCY-BASED LEARNING

Standards describe specific skills and knowledge; competencies describe broader learning goals, such as the outcomes for a unit of study, combining multiple skills and knowledge. Laura Hilger (2023) of KnowledgeWorks provides us with a starting point for thinking about the design of competency-based learning: "A standard can be most easily described as what students know—and a competency describes what students do with what they know" (p. 1). Let's take a closer look at the relationship between standards, competencies, and learning intentions.

While standards-based learning and assessment typically focus on just one content area, competency-based learning and assessment can be applicable across multiple standards and multiple content areas. Competency-based learning can also encompass both academic and personal competencies, such as the deeper learning competencies introduced in Module 3 (p. 28): thinking critically and solving complex problems; working collaboratively on complex tasks; communicating effectively; learning how to learn; and developing an academic mindset. Learning to use each of these broader personalized competencies involves applying them with academic content in real-world situations—the way a writer, an artist, or a historian would apply them. Competency-based tasks assess learning transfer and deeper understanding of the knowledge and skills described in standards, and often integrate academics with personal skills and dispositions. For example, a school with a portrait of a graduate that emphasizes critical and creative thinking assesses students' ability to apply critical or creative thinking in many content areas (Hess et al., 2025).

Standards-based tasks assess acquisition of knowledge and skills, forming the foundations for success on more complex tasks, which usually requires integrating multiple standards—such as in conducting a science investigation or writing an essay. Both of those examples apply foundational skills and conceptual understanding. Competency-based assessments can also produce student-driven evidence of deep learning in the form of authentic/real-world processes (research, investigation, composition, etc.) and authentic products (performances, podcasts, models, etc.). Table 4.3 illustrates the key differences

Figure 4.3. DOK Levels Applied to Career Pathways

Source: © Tom Mungovan (2024). Used with permission.

Stories From the Field

Teachers at the Concord Regional Technical Center in New Hampshire struggled with how to communicate to students what was required to reach proficiency for different career paths and how those learning goals related to tasks at increasingly complex DOK levels. Together, they came up with an idea that now hangs in CTE classrooms at the high school. Wall posters (similar to Figure 4.3) designed by Tom Mungovan, graphic design and creative media instructor at the school, shows stairsteps customized with skills and knowledge for each career path (health sciences, building trades, theater arts, etc.) to illustrate performance expectations with increasingly more complex skills and knowledge needed for that career.

Each "floor" shows success criteria corresponding to depth of knowledge levels leading to proficiency. This approach to communicating "I can . . ." statements to CTE students helps teachers to clarify why simply demonstrating basic skills (changing a tire, taking blood pressure, etc.) is not adequate for being fully proficient and career-ready.

The visual of a staircase leading to accomplishing more complex goals also helps students to understand what evidence of learning will contribute to demonstrating proficiency and why more complex tasks help them to build expertise in their chosen fields.

between standards and competencies in terms of scope, depth, and purpose.

In 2019, Levine and Patrick introduced seven design principles (p. 3) to guide and add clarity to the planning of instruction and assessment for schools adopting competency-based learning. Note that these seven broad principles require several shifts, such as students taking a more active role in their learning and assessment; evidence of learning, including the transfer of skills and concepts described in standards; and different possible pathways to achieve proficiency.

1. Students are empowered daily to make important decisions about their learning experiences, how they will create and apply knowledge, and how they will demonstrate their learning.
2. Assessment is a meaningful, positive, and empowering learning experience for students that yields timely, relevant, and actionable evidence.
3. Students receive timely, differentiated support based upon their individual learning needs.
4. Students progress based on evidence of mastery, not seat time.
5. Students learn actively using different pathways and varied pacing.
6. Strategies to ensure equity for all students are embedded in the culture, structure, and pedagogy of schools and education systems.
7. Rigorous, common expectations for learning (knowledge, skills, and dispositions) are explicit, transparent, measurable, and transferable.

THE BIGGER PICTURE: CURRICULUM STORYBOARDING AND TRANSFER GOALS

For many years, I worked in schools as a curriculum director and later worked with schools to help them develop curriculum. It can be a slow and tedious process, and while the resulting curriculum document might be of very high quality, it's not usually something that can be widely shared and easily understood by parents or students. An innovative approach to curriculum design is to create a storyboard that frames a narrative or a storyline about what students will be learning. Friends and colleagues Heidi Hayes Jacobs and Allison Zmuda (2023a) created this innovative process, which produces a visually appealing "story" of the learning students will be engaged with and how it applies in the real world. Figure 4.4 illustrates a sample curriculum storyboard for 7th-grade mathematics, complete with essential questions that frame the learning, success criteria (learning targets) encompassing a range of rigor (color-coded by DOK level), and real-world, kid-friendly applications of the learning. Anyone working with the related mathematics standards would confirm that this representation is standards-based and opens the door to learning transfer for students.

Figure 4.4. Storyboarding Example For Mathematics

Grade 7 Mathematics—Semester 1			
Unit 1: Proportional Relationships: Conserve or Splurge?	**Unit 2: Percentages: Make Sense of Everyday Percentages**	**Unit 3: Integers: Analyze Environmental Challenges**	**Unit 4: Expressions and Equations: Problem Deconstruction**
3 weeks	**3 weeks**	**4 to 5 weeks**	**5 weeks**

Where are we wasting water?	*How do percentages rule the world?*	*How do we interpret and model climate issues using integers?*	*How do we use equivalent expressions to simplify mathematical problems?*
We start by digging into equivalent ratios and unit rates from 6th grade to build an understanding of proportional reasoning. Our focus is to use tables, graphs, and equations to recognize and analyze proportional relationships. We then apply proportional relationships to analyze a problem about water usage.	We deepen our understanding of proportional relationships by modeling and connecting fractions, decimals, and percents. Get ready to apply your percentage skills to decode the math behind many daily realities like interest, tax, markups, gratuities, and more. Finally, tackle questions about the society in which we live by using what you've learned about increasing and decreasing by a percentage.	Math can give insight into urgent issues by objectively looking at data trends. We circle back to our initial understanding of integers from 6th grade. We then deepen our understanding of integers by using a variety of strategies to add, subtract, multiply, and divide with negative numbers. Finally, we apply what we know about integers to make sense of a climate issue.	We now focus on the analysis and deconstruction of the structure of math problems. Students make sense of verbal descriptions of situations and compare and contrast situations in similar contexts. We then build on our 6th-grade foundation of one-step equations to solve multistep equations. We use strategies such as combining, expanding, and factoring to explore the power of equivalent expressions in problem-based scenarios.
1. I can identify the constant of proportionality in tables, graphs, equations, diagrams, and verbal descriptions. DOK 2	1. I can convert fractions, decimals, and percents. DOK 1	1. I can add and subtract integers using a number line or rules for signs. DOK 1	1. I can define what equivalent expressions are and list strategies for simplifying mathematical expressions. DOK 1
2. I can plot proportional relationships on a graph DOK 1 and interpret the meaning of the points. DOK 2	2. I can solve problems involving percentages in contexts like interest, tax, markups, and gratuities. DOK 2	2. I can multiply and divide integers, understanding the rules for positive and negative numbers. DOK 1	2. I can simplify expressions by combining terms, distributing, and factoring. DOK 1
2. I can write equations to represent proportional relationships DOK 1 and explain what each part of the equation means in the context of the problem. DOK 2	3. I can explain how fractions, decimals, and percents are related and used interchangeably. DOK 2	3. I can explain whether or not two numerical expressions have the same value. DOK 2	3. I can compare and contrast different mathematical situations using equivalent expressions. DOK 2

Figure 4.4. (*continued*)

Grade 7 Mathematics—Semester 1			
Unit 1: Proportional Relationships: Conserve or Splurge?	**Unit 2: Percentages: Make Sense of Everyday Percentages**	**Unit 3: Integers: Analyze Environmental Challenges**	**Unit 4: Expressions and Equations: Problem Deconstruction**
3 weeks	**3 weeks**	**4 to 5 weeks**	**5 weeks**
4. I can explain my mathematical thinking using key words including unit rate, proportion, and constant of proportionality in the context of the problem. DOK 2	4. I can analyze how percentages affect daily financial decisions such as budgeting and saving. DOK 3	4. I can solve multistep problems involving integers in contexts, support my reasoning with calculations, models, and the chosen strategy. DOK 3	4. I can use visual representations to represent expressions, equations, and situations in context. DOK 2
5. I can determine if situations are proportional from various representations, such as real-world contexts, graphs, equations, and tables. DOK 2	5. I can model real-world situations using proportional relationships involving fractions, decimals, and percents. DOK 2	5. I can analyze data trends using integers to interpret changes in a real-world context. DOK 2	5. I can identify strategies for solving equations based on the structure of the equation. DOK 2
6. I can create mathematical models, including equations, tables, and graphs, that accurately represent proportional relationships. DOK 2	6. I can solve multistep problems involving percentages, and explain my reasoning with calculations, models, and the chosen strategy. DOK 3	6. I can model scenarios using positive and negative integers to represent changes in a real-world context and evaluate the impact. DOK 3	6. I can solve multistep equations by using strategies like combining and distributing and support my reasoning with calculations, models, and the chosen strategy. DOK 3
7. I can develop a mathematical argument to support the solution to a real-world problem applying proportional reasoning. DOK 3			7. I can write equations for complex situations, explaining my answer in context. DOK 2
			8. I can evaluate the efficiency of different strategies for simplifying and solving equations. DOK 3
			9. I can propose alternative approaches to mathematical problems using equivalent expressions. DOK 2
Standards of Math Practice: 1, 6, 7 *PA Standards and Eligible Content:* CC.2.1.7.D.1 - M07.A-R.1.1.1-5	*Standards of Math Practice:* 1, 2, 8 *PA Standards and Eligible Content:* CC.2.1.7.D.1 - M07.A-R.1.1.6 CC.2.2.7.B.3 - M07.B-E.2.1.1	*Standards of Math Practice:* 2, 3, 4 *PA Standards and Eligible Content:* CC.2.1.7.E.1 - M07.A-N.1.1.1–3 CC.2.2.7.B.3 - M07.B-E.2.1.1	*Standards of Math Practice:* 1, 3, 7 *PA Standards and Eligible Content:* CC.2.2.7.B.1 - M07.B-E.1.1.1 CC.2.2.7.B.3 - M07.B-E.2.2.1

Source: Kristina Fulton in partnership with Conestoga Valley School District, PA. Used with permission.

Articulating a unit of study or a full year's course using storyboarding has several advantages (Jacobs & Zmuda, 2023b, p. 6) and also addresses many of the design principles of competency-based learning:

- Storyboarding gives students direct access to the curriculum and supports their metacognitive understanding. They see what the curriculum is about—and their role in it.
- There is a direct impact on teaching as teachers deliberately emphasize connections, partnering with their students to awaken and discover the ideas across the flow of the school year.
- Storyboarding helps learners make sense of their experiences and see how they can apply learning in authentic ways.
- A storyboard can emphasize transfer goals, articulating how a unit is connected to long-term aims of a subject area and even the school's portrait of a graduate/portrait of a learner.

SUMMING UP

Regardless of whether your school has taken a standards-based or a competency-based approach, a thoughtful and collaborative process should be used to unwrap standards or competencies to determine *what* content students will be acquiring and understanding how (and how deeply) they will engage with that content. A cognitive rigor mindset can be used to analyze standards and competencies and to develop success criteria that might begin like "a collection of little dots" of information and lead to deeper learning, when the dots begin to connect, grow in depth and breadth as they encompass more information, and ultimately build understanding that sticks with each learner.

Individual standards or competencies are not what this is about. Curriculum storyboarding is an ideal approach to making a rigorous curriculum understandable, accessible, and transparent to everyone in the learning community, especially the students.

Applying a Cognitive Rigor Mindset to Deep Instruction

Key Questions Explored in Module 5:

- How can DOK and cognitive rigor be applied when planning learning activities?
- When a standard is based on a basic skill that only requires surface-level understanding, how can we deepen the DOK engagement?
- Is there a way to apply DOK with daily planning and not have it be too cumbersome?

I frequently introduce the concept of applying cognitive rigor to the design of deep instruction by sharing one of my favorite Sally Forth comic strips (Howard, 1991).

Comic Strip Panel 1: We see a scene at the breakfast table with Mom saying to Dad, *"Hilary's spelling test is today, Ted. Can you give her one last run through?"*
Dad responds, *"Sure."*

Comic Strip Panel 2: Dad turns to Hillary and begins with the spelling list, *"Ready? Erosion."*
"That's not the first word, Dad. How can I spell them if you jumble them up?"

Comic Strip Panel 3: Dad looks surprised. *"You only know them in order?"*
"I don't know *them—I memorized them. Nobody said anything about having to know them!"*

In 2018, Hess wrote,

> For too many years, we have equated being a good memorizer with being smart. Students knew that if they could memorize something quickly, they usually got a good grade. Class participation was praised if you were the first one with your hand up; and that made you feel really smart, smarter than most of the other kids. It felt good to be a good memorizer. Sadly, in some classrooms today, this is still the case. (p. 16)

Does increasing the level of rigor simply mean working faster, doing more, reading harder books, or just memorizing more stuff? Memorization may be efficient if you're good at it, but it is not effective if the intended learning outcome is learning transfer and deeper understanding.

Designing for deep instruction involves planning how to support students in building a foundation of conceptual knowledge and essential skills and then shifting teacher–student roles in order for them to transfer that learning to new situations. (See Module 3 for an in-depth discussion of learning transfer.) Cognitive rigor begins and ends with the student. In an ideal world, teachers orchestrate access to *time for* and *engagement with* the content so that students can move from foundational to conceptual to deeper layers of meaning. When we infuse cognitive rigor across the curriculum, it's about deciding not only what we teach, but how we teach it, how we assess it, and what we believe about our students' abilities to successfully work through challenging material. Rigorous curriculum that is not accessible to every student results in only some students developing the college- and career-readiness skills of problem-solving, critical and creative thinking, abstract reasoning, and the metacognitive skills of self-regulation and an academic mindset. If we truly believe in equity, then it's our job to collectively prepare every student to leave high school with the confidence and skills to make sense of increasingly complex (and unfamiliar) information encountered in their future lives, relationships, and work.

OPERATIONALIZING COGNITIVE RIGOR IN THE CLASSROOM

Cognitive rigor is defined (Hess et al., 2009) as encompassing (1) the complexity of the content, (2) the cognitive engagement with that content, and (3) the scope of the planned learning activities. But what does cognitive rigor look like when you or your students are actually learning? How would you describe the things you would hear and see students doing when they're thinking deeply? What kinds of materials would they be working with? How would you know that they're making meaning of the new information? These are questions I frequently ask workshop participants to think about.

Now, it's your turn—what would be on your personal list and how does it compare to your colleagues' lists? Most educators come up with many similar words and phrases that reflect six key indicators of cognitive rigor that I've uncovered in the research.

Activity 5.1: What does cognitive rigor look and sound like?

Take a minute to write down some of the words and phrases that immediately come to your mind when you think of cognitive rigor as it relates to instruction, learning, or assessment.

Are the things on your list related to the complexity of content, cognitive engagement, or the scope of the learning activity? Read the elaborated descriptions of cognitive rigor below as you consider your ideas.

Here is a more detailed description of each part of the definition of cognitive rigor.

- **Content Complexity:** The content itself has a level of complexity that has nothing to do with DOK. This includes the complexity of texts, concepts, theories, and strategies (e.g., concrete versus abstract ideas; literal vs. figurative interpretations; practical applications vs. theories). To increase access and engagement with complex content and processes, teachers need to consider a variety of strategic scaffolding strategies.
- **Cognitive Engagement:** Engagement with the content—DOK levels—describes how deeply we want students to apply their understanding to complete a task—from surface-level recall to conceptual understanding, problem-solving, or in-depth extended thinking. We know from cognitive science that emotional engagement precedes deeper cognitive engagement (Hess, 2023, pp. 13–17). When students first make personal connections to new content—"What do I already know about this topic?" or "How is this problem relevant to me/my world?"—doors to complex mental processing and problem-solving begin to open.
- **Scope:** The scope of the planned learning or assessment activity influences the overall cognitive rigor, especially when multiple sources must be analyzed and interpreted or a complex product of learning is to be developed (e.g., research project, podcast, multimedia presentation).

Watch part 1 of Karin's Master Class on applying cognitive rigor, "Are Your Students Thinking Deeply?" and compare your ideas with those of other educators. Listen to Dr. Hess summarize some of the related research—"6 Research-Based Indicators of Cognitive Rigor." You can access the video at https://youtu.be/LMDF26tAjuc.

SIX INDICATORS OF COGNITIVE RIGOR WITH INSTRUCTIONAL EXAMPLES

As you read descriptions of the six indicators of cognitive rigor (see Figure 5.1) with related classroom examples that follow, consider the Hattie (2023) effect sizes related to deep instruction.

Figure 5.1. Six Research-Based Indicators of Cognitive Rigor

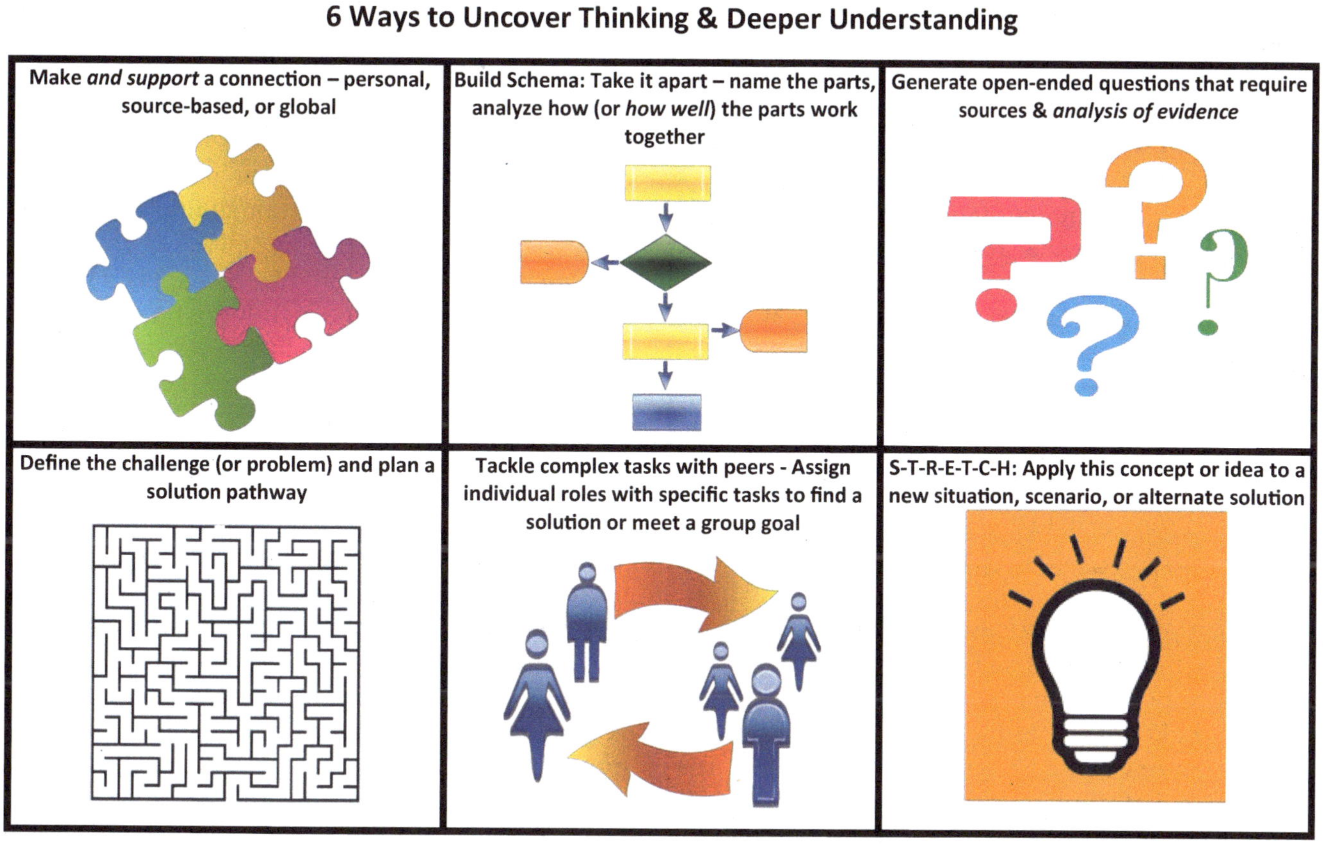

Activity 5.2: Reflect on Hattie's (2023) research

Listed below are effect sizes related to different methods of instruction (adapted from Hattie, 2023):

Cooperative learning = 0.53
Class discussions that seek & provide feedback = 0.82
Jigsaw method - peers teaching peers = 1.20
Student-centered teaching = 0.53
Concept mapping (building schema) = 0.62
Summarizing, Outlining = 0.62
Critical thinking = 0.81
Problem-based, Inquiry-based, Case-based, & Project-based learning = 0.60
Math reasoning-based problem-solving = 0.98
Science concept-based (uncover misconceptions) = 0.94
Students' ability to transfer learning to new situations = 0.86

How do these examples employ one or more indicators of rigor? Remember that 0.40 = one year's academic growth.

Cognitive Rigor Indicator 1: Making Connections is always on everyone's list. Connecting new information to prior knowledge is critical to engaging with content and sensemaking. This also relates to short-term/working memory and long-term memory and how we mentally organize new information so that it can be retrieved later to solve problems and perform complex tasks. Cognitive scientists agree that short-term memory is limited, whereas the capacity for long-term memory can be vast. Research suggests that at any given time, only about three to five disconnected pieces of information can be held in the working memory of most adults: "The actual number varies with the learner's age, type of input (factual information, visual, auditory, etc.), and the nature of the cognitive processing required" (Sousa, 2015, p. 23).

The key idea here is that

> . . . the balls of information are kept alive . . . by bouncing around the brain. The roundabout movement of the information as it's being tossed back and forth in working memory is why students can hold only so much information in their minds at once. It's like a juggler who has a shorter and shorter amount of time to grab and toss each ball . . . too many balls at once and poof everything falls away. (Oakley et al., 2021, p. 18)

When your working memory is full, you have two choices: either let go of something in order to add a new piece of information or make a connection in order to hold onto it. In the classroom, we continually introduce our students to new information. The problem is that if students are not making meaningful connections with their stored background knowledge, there is little chance that new information will ever be connected and remembered. This becomes a case of use it now or lose it (Hess, 2023, pp. 13–17; Oakley et al., 2021, pp. 18–24; Willingham, 2017, pp. 127–128).

Two important conditions have to be present to move information from working memory into long-term memory: Does it make sense and does it have personalized meaning for the learner? The first step is called "consolidation"—the new information has to connect to something a person already knows, even if it challenges something they think they know (sometimes called cognitive dissonance). Prior knowledge is a prerequisite for making sense of new learning; forming mental connections is an important task of consolidation. The brain must decide if the information makes sense. Does this fit into my current understanding of how the world works based on stored background knowledge, experiences, and perceptions? There also has to be relevance or personal usefulness to the new information. When a student asks, "How will I ever use this?," it's an indicator that the student has not had sufficient time to establish meaning. "If both sense and meaning are present, the likelihood of the new information getting encoded into long-term memory is very high" (Sousa, 2015, p. 28).

What is in your long-term memory is there because you connected it to something you already knew, you expanded upon something you knew, and you were able to internalize and apply it in ways that were meaningful to you. Information remains in long-term memory only when you periodically practice retrieving and using it. Context, such as the use of a skill or procedure in a problem-solving situation, tends to bring overall performance to an even higher level than will routine practice drills of the same skills (Brown et al., 2014, p. 81). Additionally, retrieval and more connections can be made to the stored information by using multisensory processing (e.g., related visual, auditory, or kinesthetic memories). Finally, simply *making a connection is not as powerful as being able* to *support why or how information connects.* Explanations with supporting evidence (e.g., facts, quotes, examples/non-examples, research, models) deepen the connections being made. And while having evidence is important, when students *evaluate the quality of evidence* used, their comprehension deepens and long-term memory is enhanced (Guerrero et al., 2023).

Instructional Examples: Making and Supporting Connections

- "Exit" tickets *during* a lesson: Throughout a lesson, teachers need to stop periodically—with intent—and allow all students to consolidate the learning. A general rule of thumb is that during a lesson, this should happen about every 10–15 minutes. This can be as simple as taking 30–45 seconds to turn and talk with a peer to paraphrase three key ideas, check understanding of a rule or definition, provide one example, or locate a piece of supporting evidence for a stated claim or conclusion. It's good to remember that quick checks for understanding such as these should benefit the students as much as they might benefit the teacher. [Potential for DOK 1, 2, 3]

- Sketchnoting: Sketchnoting is a form of note-taking where students transform a blank paper into a collection of purposeful doodles, text notes, diagrams, shapes, and other graphics that show visuals of their thinking (Owens, 2024). Teachers first model how to sketchnote, while thinking aloud during the lesson and pacing lessons so that students have time to stop and draw notes (during reading, viewing, listening) that *make sense to them*. Students are not simply copying the teacher's notes! Throughout the unit of study, allow time for students to revisit their sketches to revise, elaborate on, and personalize their mental maps of the information. "Part of the learning process involves students making decisions about what they deemed important enough to be recorded in the sketchnote" (Owens, 2024, p. 5). Teachers can informally conference with groups or individuals about the meaning of what is included in their sketches. [Potential for DOK 2, 3]

> **For more information and a video on sketchnoting, visit https://sketchyideas.co/what-are-sketchnotes-and-why-should-you-use-them/.**

- Say It Another Way: This is a variation of sketchnoting that builds content-specific vocabulary knowledge. Students use a simple note-taking form listing only the most essential vocabulary terms or concepts for a unit of study (one per column). Students can add other terms below each essential term (e.g., structure, function, habitat) that are related. As students work their way through readings, discussions, and other learning activities, they stop and write or sketch personalized notes under each term, using everyday, kid-friendly language (e.g., my words/pictures for structure = leg, foot, stem, root). This strategy is especially helpful for students building content-specific language skills. See Table 5.1 for an example that could be used in an algebra lesson. [Potential for DOK 1, 2]

> **Watch a short Kahn Academy video at https://www.youtube.com/watch?v=CZ5ne_mX5_I, and try sketching your notes for each essential term in the example (Table 5.1 below).** Pause the video each time you have something to add to your drawings or notes. Watching, pausing, and writing notes simulates for you how you might use this strategy with your students.

- Collaborative note-taking: Teachers can reduce the cognitive demand when understanding complex information by having students work in small groups to collaboratively develop notes using a shared outline document. This allows students to build on their collective prior knowledge and make more, and more meaningful connections to the new information through discussion and hearing the reasoning of others (Costley & Fanguy, 2021). [Potential for DOK 1, 2, 3]

Cognitive Rigor Indicator 2: Building schema involves integrating declarative knowledge (content) and procedural knowledge (skills and strategies) to figure out where there are meaningful connections, and in the process, the brain creates new neural connections, facilitating the ability to retrieve this information in the future (Hess, 2023, p. 56). When a student takes something apart and analyzes how the parts work (or do not work) together effectively, they are developing schemas for that content domain. This is the essence of critical thinking and analysis, and it's important because every content domain has its own unique schemas. Using sketchnotes, concept mapping, and graphic organizers helps students to understand both the parts and the whole of what they are learning about and how (or where) new or additional information connects.

Table 5.1. Say It Another Way

Unit: Multiplying and Dividing Powers—Integer Exponents			
List Standard/Competency: Know and apply properties of integer exponents to generate equivalent numerical expressions.			
Essential term/concept Integer exponents	Essential term/concept Properties when multiplying/dividing	Essential term/concept Numerical expressions	Essential term/concept Equivalent expressions
Your sketches, notes, highlighting, color coding, arrows, etc.	Your sketches, notes, highlighting, color coding, arrows, etc.	Your sketches, notes, highlighting, color coding, arrows, etc.	Your sketches, notes, highlighting, color coding, arrows, etc.
Unit: List Standard/Competency:			
List terms/concepts:			

Activity 5.3: Time to apply—Create a "Say It Another Way" template for a unit of study

Identify a unit of study and standard or competency statement at the bottom of Table 5.1.

List the terms or concepts that terms or concepts are the most essential for students to understand.

Add a few kid-friendly examples (words or sketches) under each essential term, thinking about how you might model this note-taking strategy for your students.

Activity 5.4: Review the strategies for making and supporting connections: Exit tickets, Sketch notes, Say it another way, Collaborative note-taking.

Which ones could you apply or adapt in your own teaching?

____

____

Instructional Examples: Building Schemas in Each Content Domain

- Find the Outlier: Build conceptual schemas having students sort and categorize information (e.g., photos, text excerpts, symbols, sounds, objects, artifacts) and defend why only some of the examples belong in a particular group. [Potential for DOK 2, 3]
- 3 Truths and a Lie: Build conceptual schemas having students write three true and one false statement about terms, events, concepts, or procedures they are learning about. Other students must detect which statement is a lie and then defend their reasoning with supporting evidence. [Potential for DOK 1, 2, 3]
- Co-developed Anchor Charts: Developing anchor charts with students helps them to understand the thought process used to locate and analyze parts of the whole: parts of an argumentative essay, steps in a math problem-solving procedure, or data collection procedures for an experiment. Anchor charts are most

useful in solidifying concepts and procedures that will be used over and over again throughout the school year. [Potential for DOK 1, 2]

- Graphic Organizers: Graphic organizers work "like a map of the content, giving students a visual, holistic representation of facts, concepts, and their relationships within an organized frame. . . . they can be used to represent abstract information in more concrete form . . . (or) relate new information to prior knowledge" (McTighe & Silver, 2020, p. 91). Organizers should be used with intent and specific to the schema being developed. A sequencing organizer can help students to develop procedural schemas for conducting investigations or solving open-ended math problems. Conceptual schemas are articulated with graphic organizers that require students to identify relationships: cause-effect, compare-contrast, problem-solution, cues for text structures, and so forth. Information can be captured in parts of the graphic organizer using words, sketches, and doodles. [Potential for DOK 1, 2, 3]

Watch a short video, "Text Complexity Toolkit," where Dr. Hess summarizes some of the related research about genre-specific schemas of text types (text structures, discourse styles, etc.). You can access the video at https://www.youtube.com/watch?v=N7weOZcC6ig&t=288s.

Activity 5.5: Review the strategies for building schemas: Find the outlier, 3 Truths and a lie, Anchor charts, Graphic organizers. Which ones could you apply or adapt in your own teaching?

____

____

____

Cognitive Rigor Indicator 3: Generating questions is usually sparked by students' curiosity, observations, or even misconceptions, sometimes resulting in further investigation. One of the best ways to shift teacher–student roles is to model for students how to ask open-ended questions that drive their own learning. Cognitive science reminds us that long-term storage of information begins with learners making connections and seeing the usefulness of constructing their own meaning (Sousa, 2022). Promoting self-directed learning skills, such as asking questions and using metacognition, empowers learners to transfer learning to new situations.

In my workshops, I often ask participants to develop basic and more complex questions for a well-known fairy tale, *Little Red Riding Hood*. Basic questions are often called closed or surface-level questions. They have one right answer and tend to be either foundational and procedural recall questions or conceptual understanding questions. "What color was Red's cape?," or "Where was Red going?," (DOK 1) or "Can you use text messages to summarize the key events in the story?" (DOK 2) are closed questions. These questions take very little time to answer (or to grade) and are a good way to quickly check understanding during a lesson. The greatest limitation of a closed question is that even if students answer them correctly, you don't actually know what students might also know beyond the answer given. I have even found that when asking students to explain how they figured out their solution, they actually got the right answer for the wrong reason!

Open-ended questions lead to broader connections and deeper understanding. They are dialogic questions, meaning that they spark dialogue and probably lead to other questions in the search for evidence: "According to the text, was the wolf clever?" (DOK 3) or "Are all wolves in literature like the wolf in this story?" (DOK 4). Open-ended questions require investigation to find supporting evidence for conclusions or claims. I always suggest using a series of probing questions—from closed to open—to move students deeper and deeper into the text or context of a problem, rather than asking one "higher-order question" and hoping that every student can get there on their own (Hess, 2023).

Activity 5.6: Observing teacher–student interactions

Using the Lesson Observation Form (Appendix D, p. 111), pair with a partner to watch a middle-school math teacher model the Notices and Wonders strategy. One person documents teacher actions; the other documents what students are doing. Then compare observations and discuss what the teacher might do next to deepen learning. Note that the teacher and student "look-fors" on this form are drawn from the Teacher–Student Roles in Table 3.5 (Module 3, p. 36).

Access the Notices and Wonders strategy at https://www.youtube.com/watch?v=yp0QORzzvSs.

LESSON OBSERVATION FORM FOR VIDEO CLIPS OR LESSON OBSERVATIONS

PART 1: Work with a partner to watch a video clip of a lesson. One person observes/notes teacher actions; the other observes/notes student actions. Describe the task students are doing. Capture *specific words* of teacher and student questions and comments.

My Notes: What the teacher did	My Notes: What students did

Instructional Examples: Generating Open-Ended Questions

- Notices and Wonders: At the start of a lesson or unit, provide complex information (without explaining it) and have students discuss what they notice and then what they wonder about the information (e.g., data table, historical photographs, contrasting media messages, art forms). Teachers are not looking for "correct" answers. Instead, they are uncovering prior knowledge and recording *all* of the students' notices and wonders. Then, as a class, they can organize or prioritize which information will be tackled first. [Potential for DOK 1, 2]
- Wonderwalls: Create a Wonderwall with the class when beginning a new unit of study or launching a project-based learning (PBL) unit with an overarching driving question. Students can generate open-ended questions, organize and prioritize them, and then select questions for their group to investigate and report on what they learned. Go to www.doinggoodtogether.org/bhf/create-a-wonder-wall to learn how to create a wonder wall with students. [Potential for DOK 1, 2]
- Send a Question/Send a Problem: This strategy promotes teambuilding using a review of what has been learned, as well as explorations that are more open-ended. Each team "puts their heads together" for a few minutes to develop a question or problem for another team to answer, solve, or respond to. Before they send it to the next team, they must draft an acceptable response to their own question. Teams switch questions and develop answers to them, and when time is called, they are sent back to the originators for feedback. Teaching students how to ask a range of question types strengthens the use of this strategy. Teams would not only be expected to answer the questions they've generated, but to teach another team how to find the answer or construct an answer if they get stuck or arrive at an incorrect solution or response. I've also used this approach for sending "evidence" to support a claim. The receiving group must evaluate the quality of the suggested evidence in supporting the stated claim. [Potential for DOK 1, 2, 3]
- TQE: Thoughts, Questions, and Epiphanies (TQE) is a student-directed method of discussing texts, developed by Marissa Thompson (https://www.unlimitedteacher.com/tqe). Cindy Dixon, a teacher in Georgia, describes in a blog post how she uses TQE in her classroom: "Students meet in small groups to discuss and record TQEs for the assigned reading, record their thoughts, lingering questions, and realizations, and generate questions they would like the whole class to discuss (posting them on a white

board). Together, the students and I choose from the submitted (posted) questions and the discussion begins. Students run the conversation by posing their questions and calling on each other. . . . My first TQE of the year begins with a short story and then we progress to a novel" (Dixon, n.d.). Teachers using TQE develop templates for individuals or small groups to use when capturing their thoughts (impressions/interpretations), their questions, and epiphanies (insights/conclusions).

An example of a TQE template might look like the one shown in Table 5.2. Students begin by individually responding to the text, then discuss in small groups, and finally discuss as a whole class. To add clarity, students highlight both the excerpt they are analyzing and each response. Individual thoughts and questions can be highlighted in one color; small-group and whole-class thoughts and questions are highlighted in other colors. Personal epiphanies come at the end. [Potential for DOK 2, 3]

The TQE strategy was originally developed to guide students in raising their own questions when analyzing print texts. It can also be used in almost any other content area with nonprint texts or a variety of other artifacts (video, websites, media messages, podcasts, music/theater/fine arts/dance products or demonstrations, case studies, observations of phenomena, political cartoons, etc.). TQE is teacher-guided at first. After students have used the process multiple times, TQE can become more student-driven. How could you use the TQE strategy in one of your lessons?

Table 5.2. TQE Note Catcher

Text:	
Text Excerpts (scan or copy/paste)	My Annotations
text with page + highlighting	My Initial Thoughts + Questions
text with page + highlighting	My Group's Thoughts + Questions
text with page + highlighting	Our Class's Thoughts + Questions
My Final Epiphanies—Insights, Conclusions, Reasoning, Reflections	

Activity 5.7: Apply TQE to a topic you teach

Think of a topic you teach and a stimulus you could ask your students to respond to with their questions and thoughts (e.g., quote, photos, demonstration, political cartoon). Describe how you envision structuring that part of the lesson and how it might encourage deeper thinking.

____

____

____

- The Depth and Complexity Framework: The Depth and Complexity Framework, developed by Sandra Kaplan, Bette Gould, and Sheila Madsen in the 1990s (Center for Depth and Complexity, n.d.), is intended to move students from beginner to expert in their knowledge of content through the use of questioning strategies. The developers identified 11 traits that experts display when deeply understanding a topic. Each trait is associated with an icon that reminds students of the approach to take when thinking through a problem or topic of study. Students can eventually use the icons to develop their own questions. For many years, Dr. Kaplan was a leader in teaching graduate courses in gifted education. I had the privilege of taking one of her courses, "Differentiated Curriculum for Gifted Students," as part of my master's program. Today the Depth and Complexity Framework is used in many gifted education classrooms but is applicable for students in any classroom. Table 5.3 provides an overview of the Depth and Complexity Framework traits with sample prompts that sometimes combine traits for greater depth or complexity. Users of this framework suggest planning lessons using a series of questions that increase in depth and complexity. For example, when analyzing characters:

Use **details** to describe a character's actions.
Compare the **patterns** in this character's actions with another character.
How would you judge the **ethics** of this character's actions?

As you read the examples in Table 5.3, can you think of a *series* of questions or prompts you might create for a unit of study using these traits? [Potential for DOK 1, 2, 3, 4]

Table 5.3. Overview of the Depth and Complexity Framework

Trait	Meaning	Sample Prompts or Questions
Essential Details	Specifics about a topic	List the important details about George Washington. Identify three details about colors used in this painting.
Language	Domain-specific vocabulary	How is Poe's language use different from Lewis Carroll's? Evaluate which author most effectively uses language to create their tone. What would happen to the tone if we used some of Carroll's language in *The Raven*?
Rules	Laws, norms, hierarchies related to the topic	Identify the rules applied in this math problem. Compare the rules Lincoln and Washington created as presidents. How would you change the rule to solve this problem?
Patterns	Things we expect to repeat	What are some observable patterns in the solar system? What patterns can you identify when analyzing [entries in your fitness journal, work samples in your portfolio]?
Trends	How something changes and the forces causing the change	How has the use of [technology, transportation, language, rules for . . .] changed over time? What are the most significant influences on those changes?
Change Over Time	How a topic has changed over time	How have the social issues in this country changed over time in response to immigration patterns?
Ethics	Problems, ambiguities, dilemmas; pros and cons of issues	Contrast the ethical dilemmas Lincoln and Washington faced. In this story, what would be the immediate effects of the children telling—or not telling—the truth? Is it ever okay to lie? What ethical issues are promoted by this source?
Big Ideas	Overarching statement: moves students away from specifics toward abstraction	What universal themes are illustrated in this [story, documentary, performance]? How can you apply this cross-cutting theme or issue more broadly? What Big Idea is the [graph, political cartoon, photograph, dance] trying to communicate?
Multiple Perspectives	Considering the same topic from different points of view	Speak from the perspective of each [character, stakeholder, player]. How and why do they each see that [detail, rule, trend] differently? Whose perspective does this [editorial, photograph, proposal] reflect?
Unanswered Questions	Things we still don't know enough about	What questions did the [author, movie, document] leave unanswered? What questions still need to be researched? What unanswered questions could this source help us with?
Across Disciplines	How this topic intersects with other fields	How does this concept or principle apply in the fields of the arts, science, mathematics, etc.?

Source: Adapted from examples at https://www.byrdseed.com

To better understand the Depth and Complexity Framework, you can find articles and videos at https://www.byrdseed.com/category/depth-and-complexity-icons.

Activity 5.8: Review the strategies for generating questions: Notices and wonders, Wonder walls, Send a question/problem, TQE, Depth and Complexity Framework. Which ones could you apply or adapt in your own teaching?

____

____

____

Cognitive Rigor Indicator 4: Defining a challenge or problem and planning a solution path is a skill that self-directed learners develop when teachers begin to let go of directing every step of the learning process. In education, we often use the meme "I do-we do-you do" to describe a gradual release of responsibility. However, many teachers struggle with that last step of letting go of control when the task is more complex than summarizing a concept or applying a routine procedure in a word problem (DOK 2). A starting point for encouraging students to plan a solution path for more complex tasks might begin with sharing examples of what the final product could look like (e.g., an infographic, podcast, a play) so that students begin with a clear picture of how and why they might apply the skills they are learning. Next, the teacher might guide students through a similar research or problem-solving process or co-develop a similar product together before giving them the final performance task to complete. (This is what I call "scrimmaging" before playing the game.) At this point, students have a clear picture of where they are headed and how they might get there. Now the teacher can ask: "What are some ways you could solve this problem/or complete this task? Brainstorm ideas with your group. What materials would you need? If you're working in a group, what will each member of the group contribute to accomplishing the goal? What steps will you take to complete this project?"

Rather than giving students the specific steps to conduct their research or develop a product, have them plan how they will do this work and submit their plan for approval. This strategy can work at any grade level, because the students don't begin the actual work until they have an approved plan. How they initially devise their plan uncovers their current thinking and allows the teacher to suggest an alternative approach or give constructive feedback to revise the plan.

Watch a short video of a kindergarten teacher guiding her students to transfer their learning about greater than/less than to plan to teach a lesson to preschool students. You can use the Lesson Observation Form (Appendix D, p. 111) to capture and discuss what you observe. Access the video, "Going Deep with Kindergartners With Problem-Based Tasks In Math" at https://eleducation.org/resources/going-deep-with-kindergartners-with-problem-based-tasks-in-math/.

Instructional Examples: Defining a Challenge and Planning a Solution Path

- Collaborative Inquiry Planning: Instead of providing specific directions for complex tasks and assigning roles, pose an open-ended problem to be solved and let teams plan how they will divide the work to accomplish the shared goal. Planning tools should ask students for the following basic information:
  - What are we trying to accomplish? (Teams restate the goal in their own words.)
  - How will we do it? What is our plan? (Teams identify steps to accomplish the goal.)
  - What will each person's job be?(Teams assign tasks to each team member and describe what each member will contribute.)

» How will we know we have been successful? (Teams describe the evidence that shows they fully met the pre-established success criteria.)

After completing the planning tool together, teachers review and approve or give feedback on the plan. Only when approved are students able to begin the work. [Potential for DOK 1, 2, 3, 4]

- Jigsaw: The jigsaw strategy requires students in a "home group" to split up the work and become expert groups, with each expert group analyzing different resources or different aspects of completing a project. Then, they return to their home groups to teach team members what they've learned and discussed so that they can integrate ideas into their own project. In project planning, each group might become experts on research strategies or different final products and come back to their group to share and decide how those products might be developed. [Potential for DOK 1, 2, 3, 4]
- Socratic Circles: Socratic questioning involves teaching students how to ask a range of questions on a topic or text (e.g., using the Depth and Complexity Framework or TQE). Students are then given time (1–2 class periods) to plan and develop questions to lead a discussion with peers, based on a given topic, problem, or issue (e.g., a case study the class is analyzing). Students need to decide what approach they want to take and what types of questions will work best to elicit dialogue and deep understanding. [Potential for DOK 1, 2, 3, 4]

Activity 5.9: Review the strategies for defining a challenge: Collaborative inquiry planning, Jigsaws, Socratic circles. Which ones could you apply or adapt in your own teaching?

___

___

___

Watch a video of 10th-graders engaging in a Socratic Circle and how the teacher keeps them on track. You can use the Lesson Observation Form (Appendix D, p. 111) to capture and discuss what you observe. Access the video "Students Cite Evidence from Informational and Literary Text," at https://vimeo.com/54871334.

Cognitive Rigor Indicator 5: Tackling complex tasks usually results in productive struggle, which can actually be a good thing when students also have "just the right" amount of support. According to Boaler (2019):

> Neuroscientists have found that mistakes are helpful for brain growth and connectivity and if we are not struggling, we are not learning. Not only is struggle good for our brains but people who know about the value of struggle improve their learning potential. . . . an international study of mathematics teaching found that teachers in Japan put their students in places of struggle 44 percent of the time in classrooms—they saw this less than 1 percent of the time in U.S. classrooms. (p. 1)

Collaborating with peers while tackling complex tasks can diminish the cognitive demand of the task without oversimplifying it. Hess and Gong (2014) found that "Collaboration and teamwork can be powerful instructional vehicles for learning . . . research suggests that these skills support creative and deeper thinking" (p. 14). Students working in a group are also developing life skills, such as "learning how to negotiate with others, how to develop leadership skills, and how to determine their own strengths so they can best contribute to the group's goal" (Sousa, 2022, p. 281).

Here's what we know about deeper thinking and putting students into groups to take on a challenging task: They can learn more complex material, they can learn content more deeply, and they can learn more quickly when they are working with someone else (meaning a peer) than when working or studying alone. Study groups organized to learn large amounts of complex college course content are a prime example of this.

It's not simply collaboration that leads to deeper thinking. It's actually dialogue that drives thinking within groups, large or small. Nottingham et al. (2017) found that

> Dialogue is one of the best vehicles for learning how to think, how to be reasonable, how to make moral decisions, and how understand another person's point of view. Research also indicates that most teachers talk too much in the classroom and don't wait long enough for students to respond. It is supremely flexible, instructional, collaborative, and rigorous. At its very best, dialogue is one of the best ways for participants to learn good habits of thinking. (p. 5)

According to these authors, here are just a few important reasons to support high-quality dialogue (pp. 6–12):

- Dialogue can develop a climate of trust.
- Dialogue gives teachers valuable insights into their students' beliefs, questions, and misconceptions.
- All students benefit from being taught *how* to think and how to develop language skills to express their ideas and understanding.
- Dialogue helps students to move from surface-level knowledge to deeper understanding of concepts.

To this list, I would also add that meaningful, collaborative discourse—especially in small, face-to-face groups—provides students with practice and models of what reasoning, giving critical feedback, and "showing your thinking" can actually look and sound like. Effective collaboration does not happen by chance. Many teachers use sentence frames and task cards to support students in knowing how to engage appropriately in small-group discussions.

Watch a video of middle school students engaging in collaborative discussions using the support of "talk move" reminders prepared by their teacher. You can use the Lesson Observation Form (Appendix D, p. 111) to capture and discuss what you observe. Access the video, "Encouraging Academic Conversations with Talk Moves," at https://www.edutopia.org/video/encouraging-academic-conversations-talk-moves.

Instructional Examples: Tackling Complex Tasks With Collaboration and Discourse

- Paraphrase Passport: This collaborative strategy is a "golden oldie" from Spencer Kagan (1992) that promotes active listening and speaking, a basic skill needed for students to work together. Use it when students work in pairs or small groups, such as to study together or to facilitate making connections in larger group discussions. Basically, when a student wants to add information or make a comment, they must first paraphrase what the last person just said ("What I think I heard you say is ___"). Then they add or extend the idea ("I think this is important because ___" or "Another reason might be ___"). Since students are bringing in prior knowledge and/or making connections using this strategy, it is likely to elicit DOK 1 or 2 thinking, encouraging near transfer. [Potential for DOK 1, 2]
- Collaborative Error Analysis: This collaborative strategy pushes students to think critically about common errors and misconceptions by creating problems with errors for peers to evaluate, solve, and explain reasoning. Chiappetta (2023) describes three rounds of the process. Round 1: Students generate a problem or open-ended response related to the current unit of study, intentionally making an error or applying a misconception. Round 2: Each group rotates to the next group, so they are looking at a problem with an incorrect solution generated by another group. Using a different-colored marker, they identify the error and resolve the problem. Round 3: Each group rotates one more time and critically analyzes the original problem and the corrected solution and determines if appropriate reasoning has been applied. [Potential for DOK 1, 2, 3]
- Collaborative Slide Decks: English teacher Marcus Luther (2024) describes how he

walks students through a sample slide deck and then gives groups control to organize their information in a collaborative slide deck, with each group taking ownership over the slide they created. "To prepare for this activity . . . I prepopulate a slide deck with relevant prompts. . . . and include a sample slide that is fully completed using a different text or situation" (p. 2). Students are given time to individually read and annotate text so that they have tangible ideas to share with each other when they meet. Sometimes the TQE strategy is used with guiding questions to focus students' thinking. When students come together, they close their computers and share their individual findings with one another before merging the most meaningful ideas and collective epiphanies. This avoids the trap of one student monopolizing what gets typed onto the team's slide. During this phase of the activity, teachers can circulate around the room and monitor progress. Slides can be created for historical context that will help students understand the text under study or break down skills needed to analyze texts. To keep students on track, a visual running timer is set for about 10 to 15 minutes. Luther adds, "Collaborative slides become excellent resources to support further learning . . . and to track growth. They also help absent students access the learning missed that day" (p. 4). [Potential for DOK 1, 2, 3]

Activity 5.10: Review the strategies for tackling complex tasks with collaboration: Paraphrase passport, Collaborative error analysis, Collaborative slide decks. Which ones could you apply or adapt in your own teaching?

____

____

____

Cognitive Rigor Indicator 6: Applying what you've learned is another example often mentioned by educators listing indicators of cognitive rigor. However, there are actually two kinds of "apply"—both are important to learning, but only one leads to deeper understanding. Let's call the lower-level type of application "practice." Learn it and practice it! Practice is important, but there is also another way to apply—this happens when you apply what you've learned to a new situation or use it for a new purpose. I've come to call this latter type of application "playing the game" after hearing Grant Wiggins (2006, 2012) refer to far transfer in this way on many occasions. You learned in Module 3 that far transfer requires a stretch beyond what has been explicitly taught. Transfer happens when you see some similarity in the situation presented and you say to yourself, "Wait a minute, maybe there is something I've done before that will work here." So you try applying what you learned in a new context. Maybe it doesn't work the first time, but you are willing to explore different possibilities and, in the process, begin to construct new knowledge, new meaning. Learning transfer builds academic mindsets, one of the six deeper learning competencies. It's taking the lower-level skills you've been practicing and putting them into play, deciding whether this is a good time to use a particular skill, testing to see what will work in this situation, and reflecting on how well it worked. Sometimes we ask our students to do all of the daily practice of skills in isolation. Then we get to the end of the unit of study and give them a rigorous assessment, only to find that they don't know how to apply what we thought we'd taught them. Maybe it's because they haven't had enough time to "scrimmage" before playing the game. Scrimmages are the bridge between the practice drills and the games. Scrimmages tell us whether students are making progress in preparing to take on more complex tasks.

TASK COMPLEXITY VS. CONTENT COMPLEXITY

Often teachers find that their units of study increase the complexity of the content without increasing the complexity of the learning tasks

Activity 5.11: Analyze a unit of study—Where are the . . . Drills? Scrimmages? Games?

Using a current unit of study, identify lessons that look mostly like practice drills, when students are applying foundational skills and concepts very much like how they were modeled during instruction. Do you have multiple scrimmages for students to prepare for a summative of assessment that looks more like a game, where skills and concepts are integrated into more complex tasks?

Are there any new strategies that you've read about in this module that you could add to the unit of study?

____

____

____

(DOK 3–4 engagement). For example, more complex texts might only be used with DOK 1–2 questions, or more complex math concepts are only applied in routine word problems (DOK 2). Remember that cognitive rigor has to balance two components: the content complexity and the task complexity. Sometimes this means that as we increase task complexity, we don't simultaneously increase content complexity. In a math classroom, a performance-based assessment (PBA) should be used with content and skills students have already mastered before introducing new and more complex content. In reading, students might use wordless books or video clips to analyze themes or character motivations before applying the same analysis skills to reading more complex texts. Imagine if at the end of every unit of study we said to our students, "Now that you've learned these skills and concepts, I want you to apply them in a new way." We would be designing units of study for learning transfer.

To illustrate the intersection of content complexity with task complexity, I frequently use the visual of two axes (Figure 5.2)—one for content and the other for learning tasks describing engagement with the content (DOK).

Figure 5.2 illustrates the intersection of content and task complexity. The resulting four task types (A, B, C, D) created by the intersection of these two axes (Figure 5.3) can be useful in guiding instructional planning and in determining the types of strategic support that might be needed as a "bridge" for student access. Those bridges will look different when scaffolding access to the content versus supporting the completion of complex tasks.

Stories From the Field

Working with text sets is one way to incorporate all four DOK levels into instructional planning, making sure that students have a chance to build knowledge and schema, and transfer that knowledge to unlock more complex texts, compare multiple texts, and write using evidence from text.

A 4th-grade teacher reflected on the patterns she saw in multiple years of state assessment data for her students. She was open to learning more about the relationship between DOK, the grade-level learning standards, and the assessment.

Starting with the Hess CRMs, she was able to see opportunities within her instructional planning to leverage the use of text sets instead of individual texts to strengthen student background knowledge and vocabulary, spark student interest in doing their own research, and make connections to the lived experiences of her students.

As we worked together to identify text sets, and the tasks that would accompany them, she had an "aha" moment. She pulled out the questions and activities that she had worked with in the past and looked at them again through the lens of DOK. When she reflected on what students were actually doing, and the type of thinking that was required, she realized that the activities were keeping students at a very surface level of understanding.

After rethinking her instructional plans, she was inviting students to deepen their knowledge and transfer their skills. —Char Shryock, educational consultant

Figure 5.2. The Intersection of Content and Task Complexity

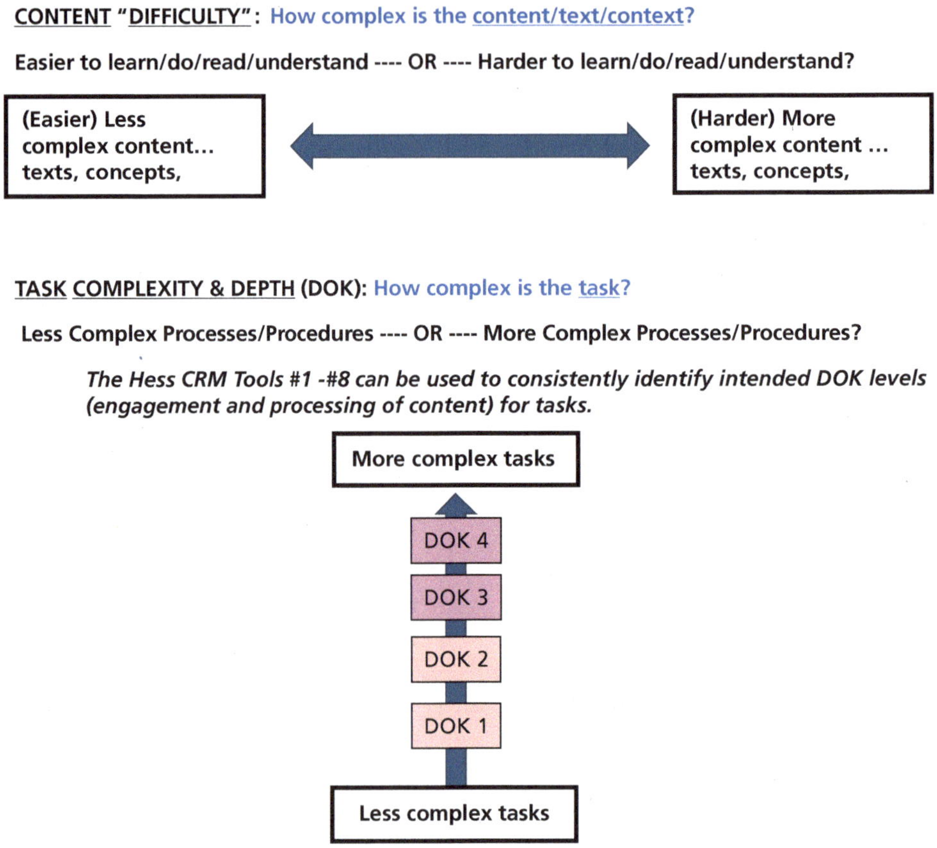

Table 5.4 illustrates differences between scaffolding access to content and providing supports to students when tackling complex tasks.

One way to increase task complexity is to "power up" the DOK 2 learning tasks in your unit. The original DOK 2 task is not eliminated but is now used as a springboard to *a more complex and empowering* DOK 3 PBA. The goal of "powering up" is not always to get to DOK 4. The more students engage with DOK 3–type thinking, the more prepared they will be for extended DOK 4–type PBAs. Table 5.5 illustrates examples of what "powering up" DOK 2 tasks could look like.

Instructional Examples: Transfer/Use Prior Learning in a New Situation

- Performance-Based Assessment (PBA) Tasks: Problem-based tasks are popular with many teachers because they generally only take one to two class sessions to complete and can easily be used within an existing unit of study. Individual students or groups can tackle a problem that requires evidence and reasoning to support a solution. Sometimes students can choose their problem-solving approach, the texts or tools they will use, or how they will demonstrate learning. In science, students might be collecting data to find out which objects are or are not attracted to magnets. They begin with a testable question, make a prediction, and collect data that either support or refute their predictions. In mathematics, students apply math skills and concepts they've been learning in a real-world problem, such as measuring angles on a treasure map to find a secret location. In social studies,

Figure 5.3. Possible Combinations of Content and Task Complexity

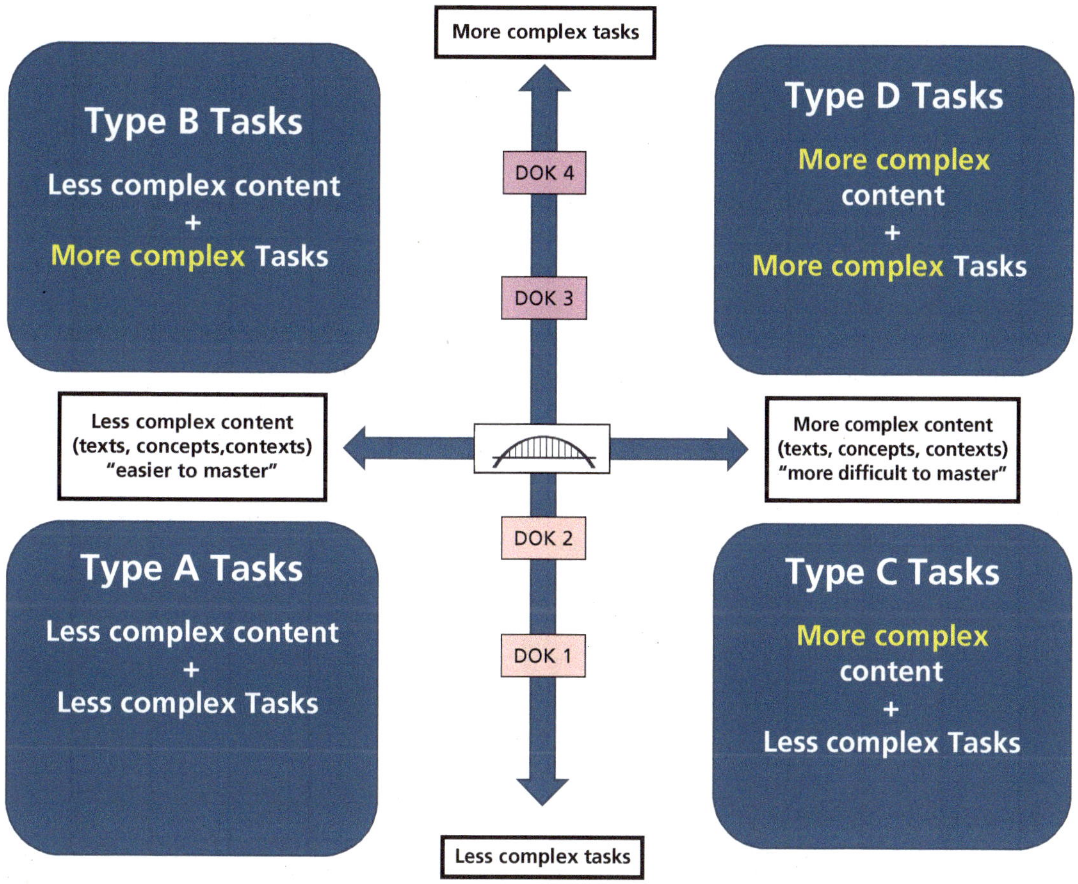

Stories From the Field

Lexie Bewley-Gilley, a high school teacher from Bullitt County Public Schools in Kentucky, was motivated to improve her final U.S. History unit of the year by applying ideas from tabletop role-playing games (TTRPGs). She recognized that content on Reaganomics and the end of the Cold War seemed disconnected to students' lives, and by her own admission, boring. So she created a multiday lesson where students "rolled up" a character who lived in the 1980s and was a part of a randomly determined socioeconomic status. Subsequent dice rolls of random economic events (based on market whims of the time period) resulted in further information about the character's life, captured on a "tracker sheet."

The result was much more innovative and memorable than before, thanks to its gamification. While Lexie already had several engaging elements of her lesson (e.g., a video created with the help of generative artificial intelligence [AI] graphics, as an AI-created narrator did a voiceover dripping in Valley Girl speak), much of the original instructional impact still hovered barely in DOK 2 territory, where the randomly determined data was dutifully collected and organized.

We worked together to make a lesson that went deeper. One improvement was to establish stopping points during the random rolling of dice for students to turn to each other for discussion, such as "How is the latest event making you feel about, and potentially shift your belief in, Reaganomics?" Another improvement was changing the expectations of the individual essay at the end of the lesson to reflect more deeply on the character's (and by extension, the student's) experience during the lesson—in particular, transferring their prior knowledge of the Cold War social studies content into a narrative from the empathetic perspective of the character. In these and in other ways, the DOK levels were significantly deepened from the original lesson plan. —Adam Watson, educational consultant

Table 5.4. "Bridging" Content and Engagement: Strategic Scaffolding Examples

Bridges to Accessing Content	Bridges to Tackling Complex Tasks
Use mentor texts illustrating clear examples	Guided practice for multi-step tasks
Design graphic organizers to connect larger concepts with supporting ideas	Model thinking "aloud" to unpack a planning-reasoning processes
Chunk longer texts and embed "stop to answer" processing questions	Access/use information in graphic organizers, diagrams, visuals
Annotate sample problems, texts, diagrams, visuals	Break tasks into steps/smaller parts with checkpoints for feedback
Embed "hint boxes" with examples, definitions, formulas, sample problems	Create "hint cards" with reminders about problem-solving or research steps
Structure group discourse to elicit prior knowledge	Annotate examples and non-examples
Lessen reading load by adding white space, color coding, key terms in bold	Structure partner and small group work
Provide context/background (video, websites, paired texts) prior to reading	Co-develop anchor charts to guide a process
Read together aloud and use audio books with turn and talk points	Illustrate/model applying rubric criteria with work samples
Use pre-post anticipation guides to elicit prior and new knowledge	Provide sentence frames to help connect ideas

students might be creating a role play based on an event in history, taking first-person perspectives of people who were actually involved in the event. Module 6 describes how to design PBAs that assess learning transfer. [Potential for DOK 1–3 or 1–4]

- Project-based learning (PBL) actually takes the place of a full unit of study, with students applying the academic skills and concepts they are already learning to investigate a real-world, driving question, such as "How can we make our community safer?" or "How can we protect important cultural places around the world?" or "How can we ensure ethical uses of AI in schools?" PBL units of study include a collaboration component, a variety of assessment types from final products to reflective essays, and a public sharing of the learning. The best free source of high-quality K–12 PBL resources can be found at PBLWorks at https://my.pblworks.org/. [Potential for DOK 2, 3, 4]

Stories From the Field

I maintain everything, and I mean everything, is about calibration. If there is a culture where people can share their work through clear and caring protocols, it is inevitable the right discussions will take place (across disciplines)—and positive change results.

I've found the use of a 4-point rubric with columns aligned to clear 4-3-2-1 DOK levels, written in a specific analytical format, can get a community around a common understanding of DOK. A common rubric design, let alone linked to DOK or not, in itself provides the opportunity to calibrate common understanding and design.

Tying disciplines to DOK criteria further lets teachers from all disciplines calibrate their perspectives. I loved seeing teachers across the spectrum share. One consistent theme surrounds difficulty, as difficult challenges do not necessarily require deep and/or rigorous thinking. The calibration efforts really brought this out. —Steve Rothenberg, former director, Concord Regional Technical Center

Table 5.5. "Powering Up" DOK 2 Tasks to Empower Learners

DOK 2 Example	Why This Is DOK 2	DOK 3 Alternative Same content, more complex task	Why This Is DOK 3
Create a "place" (city, neighborhood, amusement park, etc.) using all unit geometric shapes. Label the shapes using math terms.	Creative and engaging, but not requiring much analysis. A good review of geometric terms and figures learned.	Redesign a "place" (city, neighborhood, amusement park, etc.) for a specific (and new) purpose. Explain how the geometric shapes are used in innovative ways. Label your display using math terminology.	Creative and engaging. Requires strategic thinking, reasoning, and planning. Applies geometric figures in an unfamiliar context to solve a problem—a place for a specific purpose. Could stretch imaginations further than the DOK 2 example.
Create a presentation to demonstrate the relationships between data, sample, and statistics.	The presentation is likely to be a summary with definitions or perhaps a demonstration with examples. Although some students might take this further, it does not require analysis.	Create a presentation using a real-world context to discuss the relationships among data, sample, and statistics when designing an investigation.	Creative and engaging. Requires strategic thinking, reasoning, and planning. Applies concepts learned to the design of a real-world investigation.
Create a review game that will test your classmates' knowledge about ________. Include important facts, concepts, and related images. Provide a set of directions with your game.	Creative and engaging, but not requiring much analysis. Would likely follow a familiar/known game format. A good review of facts and concepts learned.	Create a game that will challenge your classmates to solve puzzles by combining facts, concepts, and information drawn from images. Provide a set of directions with your game.	Creative and engaging. Requires strategic thinking, reasoning, and planning. Applies concepts learned to create puzzles that use information to solve them.
Use graphic novel page panels to create text (dialogue, narration, thoughts, etc.) and images (characters, setting) that summarize the story.	Creative and engaging, but only requires depicting a series of events, explicit in the text. A good review of literary elements and comprehension.	Use graphic novel page panels to create an original text (dialogue, narration, thoughts, etc.) and images (characters, setting).	Creative and engaging. Requires developing a series of events with a story line and theme, applying knowledge of literary elements.

SUMMING UP

When we have a common understanding of what rigorous thinking can look and sound like, we can help students use a variety of strategies that build from DOK 1–2 or 1–4. Teachers who are concerned about covering the curriculum may say they do not have enough time for students to engage with complex tasks. To them I say, revisit Hattie's 2023 research. What do you see in the research that reflects your classroom? What do you see in the research that you could add—little by little—to make your classroom more engaging and relevant to your students?

As a review, watch part 2 of Karin's Master Class on applying cognitive rigor, "Are Your Students Thinking Deeply?" Dr. Hess describes how she merged two complexity models—Bloom and Webb's DOK—to create the Hess Cognitive Rigor Matix and discusses questions that are either basic or more complex. This is followed by a discussion on the mental processing needed to create as well as answer questions of increasing complexity. Access the video at https://youtu.be/NeOtmJr8Q3k.

Applying a Cognitive Rigor Mindset to Assessing Deeper Learning

> **KEY QUESTIONS EXPLORED IN MODULE 6:**
>
> - What are the "need-to-knows" for developing high-quality formative, summative, or performance-based assessments?
> - DOK 3 and DOK 4 assessments take so long. Are they worth the time?
> - How can transfer goals be used to design a performance-based assessment?
> - Does every student need to take the same assessment? If different assessments are used to assess the same skills and concepts, can I use the same scoring rubric?

At this point in our exploration of deep learning, we turn to assessment practices. A well-designed, *actionable* assessment can engage students and uncover their depth and breadth of understanding. According to Hess (2023), actionable assessments have three important characteristics: (1) assessment questions and tasks uncover what the student is thinking, not simply what the student remembers; (2) assessment evidence can be interpreted in terms of where a student is along a learning continuum to achieve a learning goal; and (3) assessment evidence can be used to provide actionable feedback to students to help them develop self-reflection skills to better understand themselves as learners, in addition to understanding the content being learned (p. 24). The instructional approaches shared in Module 5 are all examples of actionable, formative assessments, designed to uncover student thinking. As a reminder, formative assessment is as much a process or instructional strategy as it is a measurement tool. Also known as "short cycle" assessment, formative assessment practices are embedded in instruction and used during a teaching/learning cycle—to pre-assess readiness, to check conceptual understanding, to target mastery of specific skills, or to stretch student thinking. Formative assessment strategies are not limited to assessing basic skills. They can assess thinking at DOK 1, DOK 2, or DOK 3, especially when assessment tasks are performance based. Even a performance-based assessment (assessing DOK 3 or DOK 4 thinking) can be used formatively during a learning cycle as a "scrimmage" to prepare students for the final summative performance-based assessment (playing the game).

In this module, you will learn to use a set of classroom-tested assessment planning tools (found in Appendix C): Tool 9, for analyzing summative and performance-based assessments for alignment, cognitive rigor, and "fairness" for every student to demonstrate learning; Tool 10, for analyzing cognitive rigor of formative assessments and planning "next step" instructional decisions; Tool 11, for designing and analyzing scoring rubrics and assessment criteria at different DOK levels; Tool 12, for analyzing student assessment evidence and making decisions about differentiation and support; and Tool 13, for planning a sequence of assessments—formative to summative (practice drills, scrimmages, games)—that elicit evidence of learning for a series of success criteria within a unit of study.

Designing formative and summative assessments can lead to deeper learning for every student, but only when we consider each student's learning needs and how to strategically use scaffolding for different (and specific) purposes. What defines high-quality assessment?

WHAT IS HIGH-QUALITY ASSESSMENT?

We begin by looking more closely at what makes an assessment meaningful for students. Levine and Patrick's (2019) CBL Design Principle 2 states that "Assessment is a meaningful, positive, and empowering learning experience for students" (p. 3). When you think about the assessments you're currently using, do you feel like assessment experiences are meaningful, positive, or empowering for your students? Many educators would say "no." Many students experience tests and quizzes as assessments done to them, yielding a score or a grade that has little meaning, except for making them feel like either a success or a failure. However, when assessments are designed to invite student engagement, offering opportunities for them to make decisions (choice) or share their reasoning and insights (voice), students tend to take more ownership of the assessment experience. Performance-based assessments (PBAs) offer the best opportunities for deep learning and student ownership. Let's uncover the reasons why.

Activity 6.1: What is high-quality performance-based assessment?

Take about 2 minutes to brainstorm a variety of performance-based assessments that happen in or outside of the classroom (taking a driver's test, planning a family reunion, giving a demonstration, etc.). List your group's examples.

After you have at least five examples, select one and (collaboratively) answer these questions for that specific example:

A. *What skills and concepts are being measured with the selected assessment task?*
B. *What makes this a performance-based assessment?*
C. *How can best/excellent performance be differentiated from poor performance?*
D. *What makes this PBA meaningful or memorable for the learners?*

Regardless of the example chosen, all PBAs have a lot in common, even if the final products look different. Compare your responses to the above questions A–D with what most PBAs have in common.

A. With regard to skills and concepts assessed in any PBA:

- The task requires application of *multiple* skills and concepts (e.g., drawn from standards or competencies) in a new/novel context (transfer), not simple recall.
- The skills and concepts have been taught/learned and probably practiced prior to this assessment (through practice drills *and* scrimmages).
- The task requires an authentic, focused application of the skills and concepts, and is not intended to assess other unrelated skills.

B. What makes something a performance-based assessment?

- First and foremost, the task requires the student to actually *do* something, not simply describe how to do it (e.g., swimming the length of the pool versus telling you I know how to swim). There is an observable product or performance.
- Some PBAs can be done in a few hours; others may take several days to complete (e.g., project-based). Time is not the deciding factor for it to be a PBA.
- PBAs may be completed collaboratively (with a team) or individually.
- There are usually multiple steps or parts to completing the task, which result in producing a product or observable performance (e.g., gathering/processing information, deciding how to deliver the final product or performance, self- or team-monitoring progress).
- The student understands the meaning and relevance of applying these skills/concepts in a real-world situation—this is how an artist, historian, or writer applies these same skills (validity).
- The task engages the student in making decisions as to how skills and concepts *could*

be applied (while playing the game). There may be more than one approach or more than one possible final solution.
- PBAs typically assess multiple levels of cognitive demand (DOK), with a focus on applying skills and concepts through problem-solving and investigation (DOK 3 or 4).
- PBAs may be used formatively or summatively. If you didn't do it quite right, you can revise and try it again after getting actionable feedback.

C. The kind of evidence that will distinguish poor from exemplary performance in any PBA:

- There is a shared understanding (by teacher and students) about what an exemplary performance/product would, or could, look like (validity). Students understand the success criteria for completing the task and have discussed how the criteria will be applied to their final product/performance.
- A scoring guide or rubric articulates the criteria and describes indicators that will be used consistently to evaluate this and other similar performances/products.
- Multiple performance levels in a scoring rubric illustrate how a student might progress from being a novice/beginner to being proficient at completing tasks like these.
- Both the content knowledge (skills/concepts) and performance expectations (cognitive demand) are articulated in the task directions and illustrated by examples seen in student work. The use of a scoring rubric with benchmarked (annotated) work samples ensures both reliability/agreement in scoring and task validity (meaning it assesses what it is intended to assess).
- Common performance assessments, used across different classrooms/schools, provide administration guidelines to teachers in order to maintain fidelity as to how assessments are intended to be implemented. PLC teams can use student work analysis and calibration practice with common assessments to learn how to consistently interpret work quality and how to best support student needs.

D. What makes PBAs meaningful or memorable for learners?

The late, great Grant Wiggins used to administer an annual survey to students, asking them about their learning experiences in the past school year. Responses were then compiled and posted to his website. In a post on November 30, 2011, Grant reflects on one particular set of survey responses:

> One of the most interesting and revealing questions on our survey of middle and high school students involved their answer to the question: *what was the most interesting work/task/project you had last year in school?* The results were fascinating and quite helpful for teachers, particularly if you ask yourself as you read: what do all these things have in common.

Activity 6.2: What makes learning meaningful to students?

Below is a sampling of some of the more than 7,000 student responses. What patterns do you see?

To read the full post, visit https://grantwiggins.wpcomstaging.com//?s=The+student+voice+–+part+3%3A+The+most+interesting+work+of+the+past+year&search=Go.

1. **The silent Brunch i had with My American Sign Language class because we had to apply what we learned and make sure that we fully knew what we were talking about.**
2. **We did a Table setting that depicted a famous artist for my art class. It was so interesting because the final product was really cool, and I also found the process exciting!**
3. **Making ice cream in chemistry because it was something that we all like and could relate to.**
4. **The most interesting work would be actually applying what we learn, for example, we did labs in chemistry and that helped me understand more.**
5. **Last semester in sociology we got to do a project where we had to do something devious in public like be a goth.**

6. Building a house. This was interesting because I had to make something new every day and the project always had something to work on and I never got bored.
7. In the last 12 months the most interesting activity I did was make s'mores in chemistry. This was interesting because it was something fun that I enjoyed but also related to what we were learning about in class.
8. build a boat in math class for surface area and volume.
9. The baby project. We got to take home "babies" and take care of them to determine what real child care would be like at our age. I really learned that I'm never ever ever going to have a child until I'm fully ready.
10. Rank the top ten people in history from a certain time period in order of importance and do a bio on each of them
11. My favorite class project was in English when we had to remake a part of our novel into our own video project. It was awesome.
12. Create a podcast in my introduction to journalism class. It was so interesting because we had the freedom to do whatever we wanted and we still got to learn about an important part of journalism.
13. We dissected sharks. It was great hands-on experience and fun.
14. The most interesting thing was in my Advanced Studio class. All the seniors are coming together and making a memory movie of the things we did in the drama department.
15. The most interesting work that i have done was disecting a pig because it was real hands on and it shows a different perspective of things.
16. Today in history we got to talk with a WWII veteran about his experiences, and I thought it was really cool to hear his personal stories.
17. We are currently dissecting a fetal pig in Biology. It is interesting because dissections are a very good chance to see how an organism works firsthand.
18. This year, we are making a 3D to scale model of a town or amusement park in math.
19. In French when we had to do a menu on a restaurant that had to be in French. It really helped me with a lot of the food in didn't know. Also, with just how different other countries are and you can really tell by just what they eat.
20. A mock trial in my Business and Personal Law course was the most interesting work I've had to do. Not only was it fun and something very different, but it encouraged students to work hard and learn the material, which happened more than during any other time in the semester.
21. I can't recall anything considered "most interesting."

While the above ideas might not have emerged from your initial brainstorming activity, collectively they reflect what we find in the research about high-quality assessment methods.

A research summary: High-Quality Assessments (Hess, 2018, p. 135) . . .

- are defined by clear, agreed-upon expectations (standards/competencies);
- measure the individual's learning and can take different forms/use different formats;
- measure the effectiveness of instruction and appropriateness of curriculum being taught; and
- are transparent:
  - » Students know what is expected of them and how they will be assessed (success criteria)
  - » Expectations and assessment criteria are clear to educators. Ongoing training is provided as to how to teach the skills and concepts and how to evaluate the quality of evidence when scoring student work.
  - » Reports communicate information effectively to students, teachers, parents, administration, and the public at large.

Drawing from the research, I've identified seven characteristics to use when analyzing high-quality summative and performance-based assessments. I call Tool 9 my assessment *validation* tool. Validation simply means that the assessment tests what it says it will test. For example:

> ". . . to assess writing, students would actually write something. To assess history, students would actually have to construct an historical argument; while in science, students would have to design and carry out a scientific investigation. . . . if we want to know how well a student can do something we need to have them do the thing we are interested in. (Wiliam et al., 2024, p. 108)

An assessment is valid and reliable when it meets these criteria:

1. Clarity of expectations in how students will complete the task and how the results will be used.
2. Alignment to the intended content expectations (skills and concepts in standards/competencies).
3. Reliability of scoring leading to valid interpretation of results (clear scoring criteria aligned to both content and performance expectations).
4. Attention is paid to the intended rigor (in task directions, student-facing materials, texts, and scoring guides).
5. There are opportunities for student engagement, choice, and decision-making for at least some parts of the assessment (e.g., choice of topic or text; choice of approach or final product or performance).
6. Flexible enough to provide opportunities to make the assessment "fair" and unbiased for all students to demonstrate what they have learned (e.g., applies principles of universal design for learning [UDL], and allowable accommodations).
7. Clearly linked to ongoing instruction for every student (opportunity to learn).

TOOLS TO SUPPORT SUMMATIVE AND PERFORMANCE-BASED ASSESSMENT PRACTICES

Tool 9 (Figure 6.1 and Appendix C) incorporates these seven criteria using specific questions educators can answer when reviewing assessments that are currently part of the curriculum or assessments they are developing to put into use locally. This protocol is especially helpful when looking at assessments administered to all students in a grade level or course, such as a quarterly interim assessment, or when all students take a common performance-based assessment, such as a science investigation, a research project, or problem-solving tasks. Questions on pages 1–2 focus on clarity, alignment to content, alignment to rigor/DOK, and engagement. Page 3 has a checklist incorporating "fairness" indicators (accommodations, UDL principles).

Tool 9 would not be used for every summative assessment an individual teacher uses, nor for every performance-based assessment. What the tool is especially good at doing is establishing a way for teachers to calibrate how summative and performance-based assessments should be designed by every teacher in the school system.

> **Stories From the Field**
>
> When designing the Quality Performance Assessment (QPA) process used by schools in several New England states, we included use of the Hess Cognitive Rigor Matrices and Tool 9 (Task Validation) as essential tools for creating cognitively complex and rigorous assessments and curricula. The Hess CRMs helped teachers better understand how to apply DOK and design performance-based assessment tasks that engaged students in higher levels of cognitive complexity. They also helped teachers unpack and visualize how to identify different entry points and scaffold learning pathways for students. As teachers gained experience, some created student-friendly versions of the Hess CRMs, which became tools for students to exercise their agency to make choices as to how they would demonstrate their learning. —Laurie Gagnon, CompetencyWorks director, Aurora Institute.

High-quality performance-based assessments can take many forms and, at a minimum, assess DOK 1, 2, and 3 thinking. Project-based and research-based assessments typically reach DOK 4 because students are integrating ideas from multiple sources. Many teachers feel that teaching skills and concepts and then having students transfer that learning to

Figure 6.1. Tool 9, Task Validation

TOOL 9

TASK QUALITY VALIDATION PROTOCOL:
Purpose, Alignment, Engagement, & Fairness | Use for Assessment *Development* or *Analysis of Performance Tasks*

Title of Assessment/Task: Gr Level/Dept/Course/Subject:
Author(s): or Reviewer(s):
How will the assessment results be used?
(e.g., screening for placement; diagnostic to inform instruction or to provide targeted additional support; formative or interim for progress monitoring; summative for grading/report card; or other?)

Analyze and discuss each of the assessment components. Check box if there is evidence of each indicator of high-quality assessment listed. Then add any additional notes.

Clarity & Focus

☐ 1. Addresses an **essential issue, big idea, or key concept or skill** of the unit/course/discipline:

☐ 2. Directions/prompts clearly indicate what the student is being asked to do/produce

☐ 3. If parts are completed within a group: Specifies what will be assessed **individually** (e.g., projects, multimedia presentations)

☐ 4. **Assesses what is intended to be assessed** - will elicit what the student knows and can do related to the chosen standards and benchmarks. **Any scaffolding** provided (e.g., task broken into smaller steps; graphic organizer to pre-plan) does not change what is actually being assessed.

☐ 5. Is clearly linked to **ongoing instruction/opportunity to learn** (e.g., assessed within or at the end of a unit of study/course)

Clarity & Focus Notes

Content Alignment: Academic or Personal Competencies

☐ 6. Items/tasks are clearly **aligned with specific competencies/essential skills/concepts** (or intended parts or competenciess)

☐ 7. Appropriate **rubric(s) or scoring guide(s)** assess all intended parts of competencies assessed. Scoring guides are useful in determining what the student knows/does not know, not simply yield a score. (E.g., what does a score of 25 really mean? What additional or next steps in instruction does the student need? Are some rubric criteria 'weighted' reflecting greater instructional emphasis for this time of year?)

☐ 8. **Exemplars/anchor papers** illustrate expectations aligned to competencies at proficient level and performance levels above / below proficient. **Qualitative distinctions between performance levels are evident.**

Content Alignment Notes

continued...

TOOL 9

TASK QUALITY VALIDATION PROTOCOL:
Purpose, Alignment, Engagement, & Fairness | Use for Assessment *Development* or *Analysis of Performance Tasks*

Rigor Alignment/Cognitive Demand

☐ 9. Identify Depth-of-Knowledge/ DOK levels assessed/emphasized (e.g., number of score points given, weighting in the rubric). For example, an essay would mostly assess DOK 3 (full multi-paragraph composition), but also have some DOK 2 items/parts (text organization, structure) and DOK 1 (grammar, conventions) also assessed. You would check "most of the test/task" for DOK 3 and "some of the test/task" for DOK 2 and DOK 1. (See Hess Cognitive Rigor Matrix /CRM Tools for content-specific descriptors of each DOK level.)

DOK 1: Students recall/locate/reproduce: words, terms, facts; basic application of rules, procedures, which may be routine and multi-step

(☐ most of test/task ☐ some of the test/task ☐ none of the test/task)

DOK 2: Students apply level 1 within the ability to paraphrase, summarize, interpret, infer, classify, organize, compare; determine fact from fiction; solve, as in routine word problems; determine meanings in context. There is a correct answer, but may involve multiple concepts/decision points.

(☐ most of test/task ☐ some of the test/task ☐ none of the test/task)

DOK 3: Students must support their thinking by citing evidence (e.g., text, data, calculations, models). Students are asked to go beyond the text/data collection to analyze, generalize, or connect to bigger ideas. Requires 'uncovering' and interpreting less explicit knowledge. Items may require abstract reasoning, alternate approaches, inferences that connect information, application of prior knowledge or text support for an analytical judgments.

(☐ most of test/task ☐ some of the test/task ☐ none of the test/task)

DOK 4: Students use deeper knowledge of content, and evidence of complex reasoning, planning, and developing new ideas/insights/products **from multiple sources**. Usually applies to an extended task or project. Examples: evaluate works by the same author; critique an issue across time periods or research topic/issue from different perspectives; longer science/math/arts investigations or research projects involving all phases of design, testing, and refining.

(☐ most of test/task ☐ some of the test/task ☐ none of the test/task)

☐ 10. Has alignment with the **intended rigor** of the competency (or parts/combinations of the essential skills/concepts). Scaffolding does not significantly reduce cognitive demand.

Rigor Alignment Notes

Student Engagement

☐ 11. The situation/scenario or application is **authentic.** Reflects a meaningful, real-world problem, issue, or theme worth exploring.

☐ 12. Provides for student ownership, **choice, and/or decision-making**; requires the student to be actively engaged in solution finding.

☐ 13. Is administered after students have had adequate time to learn, practice, and expand their understanding of skills/concepts assessed.

Student Engagement Notes

Activity 6.3: Using Tool 9 to analyze a performance-based assessment (see Figure 6.1 and Appendix C, pp. 102–104)

To become familiar with Tool 9, read over the questions on the first two pages: Clarity, Alignment, Rigor, and Engagement. Discuss with colleagues what you will be looking for when you analyze a summative assessment or PBA, such as a writing prompt, math problem-solving task, or final unit of study product or performance.

Now practice using Tool 9 to analyze one of your local performance-based tasks What are the strengths of your PBA? Can anything be improved?

an authentic situation where they create a product or performance may not be worth the time in terms of student learning or grading. John Spencer's 2024 article, "Making Time for Project-Based Learning," describes the many fears educators express when faced with changing practices that empower their students, including that there might be chaos; students might not do the work; the change might not align with standards; students might fail the unit test; and despite their best efforts, it might not even work successfully. I think the greatest barrier might be that teachers have not seen or experienced effective models of student agency, where teacher–student roles shift, and students begin to direct their learning. These are real barriers that teacher teams need to work through when shifting to student-centered learning pedagogics. Spencer concludes with a good reminder: ". . . (this) isn't about adding something new to your plate. It's about rearranging your plate so that students work at a deeper level" (p. 2). If we also consider the impact of less traditional assessment methods on student learning, from John Hattie's research (2023), it's hard to argue against spending time on learning that exceeds an average year's growth (=0.40).

One way to manage and conserve time when using performance-based assessments is to have students work collaboratively rather than individually. Collaboration becomes a built-in support system for all learners and reduces the grading load tremendously. Scoring rubrics (discussed later in this module) can be designed so that parts of the project are graded on collaboration skills—how well students work together to complete a task—and other parts are graded on individual contributions to the products the group creates.

Hattie Effect Sizes (2023)—Assessment Methods

Success criteria = 0.64
Students' ability to transfer learning to new situations = 0.86
Student self- and peer-grading = 0.54
Seeking help from peers = 0.68
Mastry learning = 0.67
Service learning = 0.53
Performance-based assessment (presentation, portfolio, project) = 0.67
Student self-judgment and reflection = 0.81
Self-reporting grades (e.g., student-led conferencing) = .96

Guidance for "Balancing DOK Levels" in Summative Assessments

1. *A summative assessment should not look like a game of* Jeopardy!, *with dozens of low-level, recall questions.* You've already asked most of those questions on quizzes and homework assignments. As I once told a group of high school English teachers who had 50 multiple-choice (DOK 1) questions about *Romeo and Juliet*, "Get rid of 35 of them and ask one or two open-ended questions that truly assess the meaning a reader can gain from reading this play. Then assign those 35 test points to the essay responses, putting greater emphasis on interpretation than on recall." Only about 5% of a summative assessment should include basic DOK 1 questions.
2. *About 40%–50% of the test points on a summative assessment should focus on DOK 2, conceptual understanding.* These questions would include explaining relationships, identifying central ideas, solving routine word problems, identifying trends in data, and so forth. McTighe and Silver (2020) identify seven thinking skills that help students to "achieve deep and lasting learning by facilitating acquisition of information for greater retention and retrieval, fostering active meaning making that leads to deeper understanding of 'big ideas,' and building the ability to apply, or transfer, learning to new situations both within school and beyond" (p. 2). These seven skills mostly require DOK 2-type thinking and prepare students to transfer learning to more complex, nonroutine scenarios: conceptualizing, note-making and summarizing, comparing, reading for understanding, predicting and hypothesizing, visualizing and graphic representation, and perspective-taking and empathizing. Perspective-taking and empathizing build on conceptual understanding and are best assessed with open-ended questions requiring students to construct (rather than select) a response.
3. *To assess thinking of younger students and students with limited communication skills, use scribing or 1-on-1 conferencing.* The best, and perhaps the only, way to assess reasoning and thinking with young children is to observe them while they work, ask probing questions that get to the reasoning they're using as they work, and scribe their exact words to capture their thinking. Scribing is critical to student work analysis at the younger grades. A related discussion follows when we we explore uses of Tool 12 (student work analysis).
4. *Think of DOK as a ceiling, not a target,* when developing assessments. Hess (2021) explains that

> A DOK "target" has a narrow focus (e.g., only assessing DOK 2-type thinking), whereas a DOK "ceiling" is the highest potential depth of knowledge level to be assessed, as well as assessing DOK levels up to the ceiling. The DOK ceiling is determined by the intended cognitive demand of the *combination of skills and concepts* (standards/competencies) assessed, such as in a PBA. When only the highest DOK level is assessed as a target—only DOK 3 or DOK 4 are assessed—the assessment as a whole may end up being too difficult for many students, and important information about learning along the achievement continuum would be lost. (p. 19).

See Table 6.1 for an example of DOK ceilings and targets.

5. Scoring rubrics can be designed to assess a range of DOK levels for more complex tasks, with more score points attributed to questions asking students to construct knowledge or share new insights—questions that require learning transfer. This is how you balance a summative assessment using fewer questions, each receiving more score points (about 35%–40% of the total).

Watch Part 4 of Karin's Master Class on Applying Cognitive Rigor, "Are Your Students Thinking Deeply, or Just Working Harder?" Dr. Hess discusses "balance" in summative assessments and using simple grading scales for open-ended questions (11:17 minutes). Access the video at https://youtu.be/cGTBDFRo200.

DESIGNING PBAs TO ASSESS LEARNING TRANSFER

Hess (2023, pp. 96–97) identifies seven common characteristics of high-quality PBAs. The first four focus on deep, authentic, performance-based learning; the last three push students out of their comfort zones, requiring transfer and constructing of knowledge. All final products are not expected to look alike; however, they can be assessed using similar success criteria.

1. PBAs have open-ended contexts. Prompts or situations posed to students are open-ended and guided by essential or driving questions.
2. PBAs productively challenged students. Searching for answers to an essential question causes students to grapple with concepts and test different approaches, and it stretches their thinking.

Table 6.1. An Example of DOK Assessment Ceilings and Targets in Reading

One State's Reading Standards	DOK Ceiling	Potential DOK Levels for Assessment
R3: Applies word identification/ decoding strategies by . . . R3: 3b Identifying multisyllabic words (e.g., "pretending," "discussion"), by using knowledge of sounds, syllable types, or word patterns (including prefixes, suffixes, or variant spellings for consonants or vowels, e.g., bought)	1	1 (Applying knowledge of sounds, syllable types, word patterns)
Students identify the meaning of unfamiliar words by . . . **R5: 5a** Using strategies to unlock meaning (e.g., knowledge of word structure, including prefixes/suffixes and base words; or context clues; or other resources, such as dictionaries or glossaries; or prior knowledge)	2	1 (Applying knowledge of word structure) 2 (Using context clues and resources such as dictionaries to unlock meaning)
R13: Analyze and interpret elements of literary texts, citing evidence where appropriate by . . . R5: 13a Making logical predictions R5: 13b Describing characters' physical characteristics, personality traits, or interactions; or providing examples of thoughts, words, or actions that reveal characters' personality traits or their changes over time R5: 13c Making inferences about problem, conflict, solution, or the relationship among elements (plot, character, setting) within text (e.g., how setting affects a character or plot development) R5: 13d Identifying author's message or theme (implied or stated, as in a fable)	3	1 (Describing characters' physical characteristics, thoughts, words, or actions) 2 (Predicting a logical outcome; making inferences about problem, solution, or conflicts) 3 (Identifying author's message or theme using supporting evidence from text)

Source: Adapted from Hess (2013). Used with permission.

3. PBAs uncover thinking. Products, performances, and self-reflection activities engage students in substantive reasoning related to making connections among concepts, theories, and the real world.
4. PBAs promote authentic doing and sharing. Students apply real-world skills and dispositions to develop products and performances.
5. PBAs stretch thinking and integrate academic knowledge and personal skills with student input. Student input can include anything from making choices about content or strategies to be used, who they will work with on the task, and how they will reflect on processes used. Both products and processes are considered in the final evaluation of PBAs.
6. PBAs stretch student thinking and require far transfer. Students integrate and apply skills and concepts learned when solving real-world problems.
7. PBAs spark reflective and metacognitive thinking. Unlike traditional tests, asking students to share how they learned is as important as asking what they learned.

Using The S-T-A-R-S Protocol: Choice and Voice in The Design of PBAs

For many years I've worked with schools to develop performance-based assessments. It is not an easy process—to come up with ways to integrate multiple skills and concepts, provide opportunities for inquiry and critical and creative thinking, and still maintain alignment with the intended content standards or competencies being taught. I eventually figured out that student input was also essential to the design process. This is another example of teacher–student shifts in roles supporting deeper learning. Working with cohort groups from Chicago-area schools over several years, teachers tested out my S-T-A-R-S protocol to design a PBA they could use within a unit of study that transferred what students were already learning and allowed for student choice and voice. I call my evolution from teacher-designed to teacher–student-designed PBAs "PBA 3.0." PBA 1.0 was when I did all of the designing of engaging projects, but rarely captured high-quality evidence of learning. PBA 2.0 was when I still did all of the designing but allowed some flexibility for choice and had clear scoring rubrics, and sometimes even exemplar products, to share with my students to clarify expectations. PBA 3.0 invites students into the design process, offering choice and authentic voice, and assesses not only the resulting products but the processes of learning.

> **Watch a short video, "Karin Hess's 'Handy' Brain Model,"** where she explains PBA 3.0 and the cognitive science underlying engagement leading to greater ownership of the learning when students become co-designers of PBAs. Access the video at https://www.youtube.com/watch?v=DrGggsJWgQk.

I developed S-T-A-R-S (Hess, 2021) as a process to help teachers think through how students would transfer their learning to the real world and how students would intensionally be given decisions in how they would accomplish the tasks. S-T-A-R-S is an acronym used in planning the PBA. Below is a short description of each part of the protocol.

- **S**cenario or **S**ituation—Describe a real-world context for a problem, a challenge, or a complex task to be completed that is appropriate for transferring skills and concepts. Is this how a scientist, artist, or mathematician might use these skills and knowledge?
- **T**ask(s) or investigation to be completed or problem(s) to be addressed.
- **A**udience—who the information will be shared with (peers? others?).
- **R**esources needed/available to complete the task and **R**oles for individuals or team members.
- **S**uccess Criteria for **S**elf-Assessment are used to develop self-reflection questions and scoring rubrics. Three components of success criteria are:

- **Content:** Major concepts, principles, or theories to demonstrate understanding and make broader connections to Big Ideas/Essential Questions/Driving Questions
- **Processes, skills, and thinking strategies** (engaging with content) applied to complete the task(s), such as research, data analysis, creative problem-solving, design thinking, drafting a blueprint, etc.
- **Product(s)** that show evidence of what was learned (e.g., performance, product, model, teach/inform/engage others, propose or test a solution)

In the S-T-A-R-S planning template, skills, concepts, and products fall under "success criteria" because students will be assessed, in part, on their knowledge related to skills, concepts, and products created to demonstrate their learning (See Figure 6.2.).

S-T-A-R-S planning begins by asking teachers, "What are you already teaching—what skills and concepts are students learning now that they could apply/transfer in a novel, real-world situation?"

For example, if students have learned about a major event in history, then knowledge of that *content* might be what students transfer to a novel context, such as applying what they've learned about Franklin Delano Roosevelt's New Deal to a present-day context. Or, if students have learned a *process/procedure*, such as statistical analysis, they might transfer those skills to a novel context, applying statistical analyses to determine appropriate versus inappropriate data use by today's media.

To develop the prompt for the PBA:

1. Identify the essential *content* or *processes* students are currently learning (or have learned) and consider how they might apply them in an authentic/real-world context. If students have learned how to develop a specific type of *product* (e.g., model, infographic, essay) that you want them to use in the transfer task, list that, and any content or processes under "success criteria" headings in the planning template. (See Figure 6.2.)
2. Next, describe a real-world scenario where students will apply their learning in a new situation and a task to be completed.
3. Decide on areas where students have input into the overall task design, adding "?s" in the table to indicate *decisions or choices students must make* as part of the task design process.
4. Use information in the planning template to develop a prompt for the PBA.
   For example: We have been learning about ________. Now you will have a chance to apply that learning in a new situation by _______. You will need to decide ______. Your final product should include ______________________.
5. Introduce the PBA prompt to the class, discussing what they have been learning, decisions they'll need to make, and how they will now transfer that learning to a new situation.
6. Use the PBA prompt to develop a scoring rubric. Tool 11 (Appendix C, p. 106) includes guidance for developing rubric language describing each performance level.

Activity 6.4: Analyze sample PBA prompts and then create your own prompt

Read the two PBA prompts below and identify the scenario, the task to be completed, the knowledge to be transferred, and the product to be developed. In each PBA, what decisions will students need to make?

Then develop a prompt for your PBA using the S-T-A-R-S planning protocol. (Table 6.2)

For more examples, watch a webinar of the 2023 Showcase where teachers describe their PBAs at https://edsystemsniu.org/performance-based-assessment-showcase/.

Table 6.2. The S-T-A-R-S Planning Template with Examples

S Scenario or Situation	T Task	A Audience	R Resources and Roles	S Success Criteria for Self-Assessment Learning to Transfer		
Describe a real-world situation	In this task, you will . . .	Who will you share this with?	What resources are needed? What is your role?	Content/ concepts Big Ideas	Processes and skills	Product(s) of learning
Plan an event or class trip	Determine how much it will cost and a plan to earn a given amount of money.	Convince the class your plan is the best plan	?	?	Decide how to research ideas. Create spreadsheet.	Business plan with data, timeline
A Design Challenge	Build or create a better way to_____	?	?	?	Plan, design, collect, and analyze data	Build, test, and refine the prototype
Solve a Multistep Problem	Redesign a floor plan with these criteria: Develop a thematic banquet menu.	?	?	?	?	Present budget and design in support of proposal
Our school has large numbers of things—chairs, books, students	Figure out a strategy to count a very large number of things.	Peers	?	? (Choose what to count)	Counting strategies and estimation	Demonstration
Do you see the potential for a dystopian society right now?	Identify and describe a real-world dystopia.	?	?	Dystopian literature	?	Choose infographic or podcast

PBA Example 1

The media often skews data to sway viewers to think about a specific topic in a certain way, leading to media bias. Now you'll have the opportunity to analyze data presented in an article or media message. You will . . .

1. Evaluate the given datasets provided to form your own opinion about any false biases presented in the message.
2. Use knowledge of statistics and proportional reasoning to disprove/prove potential biases of the article.
3. Write a letter (to the author/media outlet) to justify your opinion using the data/math as evidence for your claims.

PBA Example 2

We've been learning about how authors use rhetorical strategies to communicate a message. Now you'll apply what you've learned and incorporate the use of rhetorical strategies to develop either an original advertisement, a speech on a debatable issue, or a debatable scientific treatise. The final product will be critiqued by your peers. Finally, you'll write a reflection evaluating the effectiveness of the strategies you used.

TOOLS TO SUPPORT FORMATIVE ASSESSMENT PRACTICES AND LESSON PLANNING

Now that you have developed a PBA prompt to use near the end of a unit of study, it's time to think about how you'll prepare students for that PBA. Remember, the PBA is the game, and now you need to think about developing drills and scrimmages to prepare for that game.

The remaining three tools can be used to support day-to-day formative assessment practices and lesson and unit planning that build deeper thinking along the way. Directions for using Tool 10 (Analyzing Formative Assessments), Tool 12 (Student Work Analysis), and Tool 13 (Lesson and Unit Planning Template) are included on each tool, so the instructions that follow here are brief. All of these tools are unique in that they include the application of DOK-types of thinking to consider when planning for deep instruction.

> **To better understand purposes of formative assessment, view Dr. Heidi Andrade (2016) in a video clip,** "Arts Assessment *of* and *for* Learning" at http://artsassessmentforlearning.org/about-assessment.

Tool 10: Analyzing Formative Assessments (Appendix C, p. 105) was designed to reflect best practices in formative assessment, using assessment results to make decisions about next steps for instruction. In addition to alignment with standards and learning targets (success criteria), this tool includes three unique analysis features (Figure 6.2) related to applying cognitive rigor.

> **STORIES FROM THE FIELD**
>
> I use these tools (10 and 13) a lot when I am planning with second- and third-year teachers to help them scaffold lessons and build towards a task or PBA. I also have new teachers use a blank rigor matrix to build units (lesson by lesson) toward the PBA so they can see how learners build capacity and give clarity to the purpose of each lesson.
>
> These tools help the new teacher see how review of past information builds stickability with new information and skills. Using this process, students build confidence in the learning and want to learn more.
> —Kirsten Soroko, Pinkerton Academy, New Hampshire

Figure 6.2. Unique Analysis Features of Tool 10

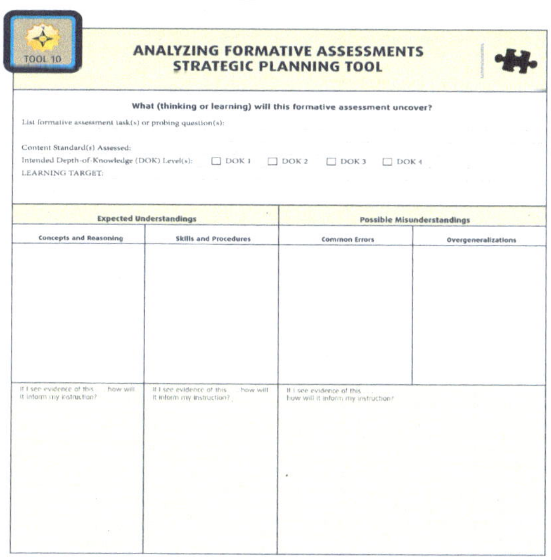

TOOL 10

ANALYZING FORMATIVE ASSESSMENTS
STRATEGIC PLANNING TOOL

What (thinking or learning) will this formative assessment uncover?

List formative assessment task(s) or probing question(s):

Content Standard(s) Assessed:
Intended Depth-of-Knowledge (DOK) Level(s): ☐ DOK 1 ☐ DOK 2 ☐ DOK 3 ☐ DOK 4
LEARNING TARGET:

Expected Understandings		Possible Misunderstandings	
Concepts and Reasoning	Skills and Procedures	Common Errors	Overgeneralizations
If I see evidence of this ___ how will it inform my instruction?	If I see evidence of this ___ how will it inform my instruction?	If I see evidence of this ___ how will it inform my instruction?	

Unique Analysis Features of Tool 10

- Identify the types of thinking you are assessing—routine skills (DOK 1, DOK 2), conceptual understanding (DOK 2), or reasoning and problem solving (DOK 3).
- Identify any possible errors you *anticipate seeing* in routine skills (DOK 1, DOK 2); identify possible overgeneralizations/misconceptions you might see in concepts (DOK 2) or reasoning (DOK 3).
- If there is no reasoning question, add one to the assessment (e.g., is your solution reasonable?). Explain your thinking.
- Formative activities should be actionable and uncover thinking. Depending on what you see in student work, what instruction will support next steps in learning?

Tool 12: Student Work Analysis (see Figure 6.3 and Appendix C, pp. 107–108) is used as a quick sorting activity for short-cycle assessment tasks. Remember that short cycle includes tasks such as open-ended conceptual questions, problem-solving tasks, error analysis tasks, or short writing prompts. After students have completed the task, teachers sort student papers into two piles: students who met all objectives and students who did not meet all objectives. A second sorting is then done with each of those piles. For students who have met all objectives, work samples are sorted into "met the objective" and "went beyond meeting the objective." For students who did not meet the objective, some papers are placed in the "almost met the objective" pile, and the rest are put into the "just getting started" pile. Now teachers use a three-step "D-I-E" process:

- *Describe* typical performance of students in each of those categories: getting started, getting close, met the objective, and went beyond the objective.
- Using descriptions of what was observed in student work, *interpret* what students know and what students need next.
- Finally, *evaluate* actions the teacher will take to support student learning, such as differentiating instruction for targeted groups or whole-class reinforcement of skills.

Watch the video, "What Can We Learn From Analyzing Student Work?" illustrating the student work analysis process in action using Tool 12.

[Part 1] Dr. Hess explains her D-I-E approach to analyzing student work at https://www.youtube.com/watch?v=lwXcm1rbtFk (8 minutes).

[Part 2] Dr. Hess walks teachers through how to complete the student work analysis (note that in the video, this is numbered Tool 11 but is identical to Tool 12) at https://youtu.be/w3l47rq6nBI (9 minutes).

[Part 3] Dr. Hess guides teachers in analyzing student work from a kindergarten math problem-solving PBA at https://youtu.be/7JttirFB5ak (19 minutes).

[Part 4] Dr. Hess guides teachers in analyzing student work from a grade 3 writing PBA at https://youtu.be/wjuDs5N7LDs (16 minutes).

Figure 6.3. Student Work Analysis for Planning Next Steps in Instruction

TOOL 12

STUDENT WORK ANALYSIS
Analyzing and Acting on Evidence

Subject Area: **Grade Level:**
Unit/Topic: **Performance Task:**
How used? ☐ Pre/formative ☐ Mid/Interim ☐ Post/Summative
Date administered:
Content Standards Assessed:
Intended Depth-of-Knowledge (DOK) Level(s): ☐ DOK 1 ☐ DOK 2 ☐ DOK 3 ☐ DOK 4

☐ 1. **Using district or classroom assessment or rubric, describe expectations for performance.** (See wording of prompt, standards-specific rubric, Hess CRM, and/or standards to determine desired expectations.)

☐ 2. Quickly "sort" students' work by degree of objectives met. List student name or % in each category so you can track progress over time with each major assessment. (a) **Start by sorting two larger piles: met or not met.** You may also need a "not sure" pile at this point. (b) **Re-sort each pile**: not met partially met but close vs. minimal; met met vs. met plus more. (c) **Distribute any remaining work samples** by matching them to typical work from each set.

This is not scoring!

Objectives not met	Objectives partially met	Objectives fully met	Objectives fully met and exceeded
% of class	% of class	% of class	% of class

continued...

TOOL 12

STUDENT WORK ANALYSIS
Analyzing and Acting on Evidence

☐ 3. **DESCRIBE:** Choose a few work samples from each group or category and **describe** "typical" performance for most of these students or describe the specific performance of selected students in each group

Objectives not met	Objectives partially met	Objectives fully met	Objectives fully met and exceeded

☐ 4. **INTERPRET:** Consider the next steps for instruction based on your **interpretation of the learning needs** of students in each targeted group and the overarching learning goals. **List learning needs below**

Objectives not met	Objectives partially met	Objectives fully met	Objectives fully met and exceeded

☐ 5. **EVALUATE and PLAN:** Identify differentiated tasks or strategic scaffolding strategies to move **targeted groups or ALL** students forward. Note any whole-class or small-group patterns or trends.

Instruction for all students:

Targeted instruction for some students:

Source: Hess (2013). Used with permission.

Figure 6.4. Lesson and Unit Planning Template

TOOL 13

RIGOR BY DESIGN
LESSON AND UNIT PLANNING TEMPLATE

Unit or Project: Grade Level:

Essential or Driving Question (Big Idea):

DOK Levels	Teacher Roles	Planned Strategies Observable Evidence	Student Roles	Observable Evidence of Learning
1 **Acquire Foundation**	☐ Questions to focus attention (*Who? What? Where? How? When?*) ☐ Directs, leads, demonstrates, defines ☐ Monitors practice ☐ Scaffolds for access and focus		☐ Acquires vocabulary, facts, rules, routines ☐ Memorizes, recites, quotes, restates ☐ Retrieves information, uses required tools and resources ☐ Practices and self-monitors routine skills ☐ Seeks support, asks questions to clarify procedures or task expectations	
2 **Use, Connect, Conceptualize**	☐ Questions to build schema: differentiate parts from whole, classify, explain relationships (*Can you explain examples/ non-examples? Cause-effect?*) ☐ Draws out basic inferences ☐ Models/scaffolds conceptual understanding (*Why? Under what conditions?*) ☐ Provides guided practice for multi-step tasks		☐ Explains relationships, sorts, classifies, compares, organizes information, summarizes ☐ Makes predictions based on estimates, observations, prior knowledge ☐ Proposes problems, topics, or questions to investigate ☐ Raises conceptual questions (*Why? What if?*) ☐ Selects tool or strategy for specific purpose ☐ Follows teacher-designed procedures	
3 **Deepen & Construct Meaning**	☐ Questions to probe reasoning, thinking, planning (*How will you know or do this? Where is the evidence?*) ☐ Promotes peer discourse & self-reflection to uncover Big Ideas, themes ☐ Designs tasks requiring proof, justification, analysis of evidence quality and accuracy ☐ Models/scaffolds validating sources ☐ Supports student-designed performance tasks		☐ Uncovers relevant, accurate, credible information, flaws in a design, or proposed solutions linked with Big Ideas, themes ☐ Raises questions that explore underlying meanings (*Is this what the author is saying? What can we learn from this?*) ☐ Plans how to develop supporting (hard) evidence for conclusions, solutions, or claims ☐ Researches, tests and revises ideas, solves non-routine problems ☐ Sets goals, monitors progress ☐ Self-assesses; uses feedback to improve quality	
4 **Extend, Transfer, Broaden Meaning**	☐ Questions to challenge or to extend meaning (Big Ideas, themes), explore sources, broaden perspectives (*Are there potential biases? Can you propose an alternative model?*) ☐ Models/scaffolds triangulating sources, peer-to-peer critique, self-reflection ☐ Supports student-designed performance tasks ☐ Promotes peer discourse & self-reflection to uncover Big Ideas, themes		☐ Initiates, transfers, and *constructs* new knowledge, insights linked to Big Ideas, themes ☐ Modifies, creates, elaborates based on analysis and interpretation of multiple sources ☐ Raises novel questions and investigates real-world problems and issues ☐ Sets goals, monitors progress ☐ Self-manages time ☐ Generates self-reflections; self-asesses and uses feedback to improve quality	

Source: Hess (2013). Used with permission.

Tool 13, Lesson and Unit Planning Template (Appendix C, p. 109), can be used to analyze existing units of study or to create units of study using a series of increasingly more complex success criteria (Figure 6.4). This tool operationalizes the teacher–student roles during instruction that have been previously discussed in Modules 3, 4, and 5. It can also be used to analyze an observed lesson, using notes from an observation to discuss what students were doing and talking about during the lesson and determining how to deepen the learning in the next lessons.

Activity 6.5: Choose either Tool 10 or Tool 13 and use it to analyze a formative assessment strategy you currently use or the flow of lessons in one of your units of study

What are you learning? How could the task or the lessons be revised to be more rigorous and engaging?

SUMMING UP

Throughout these modules, I've been stressing that rigorous learning doesn't happen by chance.

Stories From the Field

I worked with a middle school teacher whose 8th-graders were learning about the impacts of westward expansion in the United States: economic and industrial development, debates over sectional issues, War with Mexico, and the displacement of Native Americans. The unit of study focused on two standards.

The teacher's PBA asked the class to create a scenario that depicted America as if the people on the West Coast of America at the time decided to do eastward expansion instead of the westward expansion that actually took place. Using my process of solution-centered mindset (SCM), students had to follow (transfer) the focus of the standards:

1. Account for the various treaties and purchases during this time period.
2. Show how economic and industrial development may change.
3. Discuss the alternate outcome of the War with Mexico.
4. Provide an idea of a better way to work with Native Americans.

How they presented the new expansion was determined by the students. The students had to show how westward expansion happened, considering each of the limiting factors, then show how they changed, and account for that in modern America. For example, how would the eastward expansion be able to acquire the Louisiana Territory?

The level of critical and creative thinking during lessons leading up to and including the performance-based assessment provided opportunities for students to reach deeper levels of understanding of the social studies standards and make personalized decisions along the way. —Norm Potter, author, educational consultant

Educators must develop a shared understanding about how they will support student learning that is deeper and more meaningful than it has been in the past. The learning environments that we create in our schools need to invite *all* students to actively participate and take more ownership of their learning. Collaborative, inquiry-based experiences—applied to the real world—add relevance and require that the traditional teacher–student roles shift, making students co-designers of the learning.

The focus of learning should be less on grades and more on authentic representations of what students know and can do. Performance-based assessments are the best way to represent deeper learning, but they require planning and targeted support along the way. Formative assessments must be designed to uncover student thinking so that appropriate supports can move learning forward. The work we ask our students to do should be both meaningful and of high quality.

Ron Berger, senior adviser of teaching and learning at EL Education, speaks eloquently about the importance of rethinking the role of students, and the powerful impact of guiding students to create high-quality, meaningful work, what he defines as *beautiful work*:

> When you're proud of your work, when it's beautiful, you're motivated to work harder. Kids practice their gymnastics, practice their flute, practice their soccer skills because they want to be great. Not to be proficient. . . . And I feel like that's what school should be about. It should be inspiring kids to want to be great. . . . Seeing kids do beautiful work and recognize beautiful work in each other. (As cited in Gonser, 2021)

In a 2016 interview, Berger suggests,

> [S]tart small and do some really powerful, complex and beautiful work with kids that they can share with their families with pride, and that you can share with the community with pride and build from that. . . . maybe a project where students identify an environmental problem in the community, do data collection, write up a scientific report, bring in scientific experts to critique it, and read real scientific papers. Crucially, there should be time to reflect, incorporate feedback, and turn in multiple drafts. That alone could change the whole school experience for those kids. . . . it's not totally project-based learning; it's not scary. But once you've done that, then the parents and kids are proud to have done something much deeper and more complex and challenging. (Schwartz, 2016, p. 3)

Suggested Responses to Guided Activities

A.1. Suggested Responses for Table 1.3, Analyzing the Intended DOK Levels of Learning or Assessment Tasks

Task Examples	Intended DOK Level?	What mental processing is called upon to complete the task?
5. Create a booklet of ______. Include illustrations, a description of attributes, and other identifiable information for each example.	1	**This is mostly looking up and putting together a collection of facts and details. While perhaps engaging and creative, it does not require strategic thinking, extensive planning, or tying ideas together with an underlying theme.**
6. Compare and contrast two novels written in about the same time period and determine which version is the most historically accurate. Use evidence cited in the texts and other sources to support your conclusions.	4	**Requires comprehension of multiple sources for locating evidence. Requires support for conclusions drawn from at least two texts.**
7. Explain the difference between a ratio and a proportion. Provide examples and non-examples of each to support your explanation.	2	**This is likely to be a summary with definitions and examples, but does not require any analysis; requires making connections.**
8. Evaluate the historical accuracy of a novel you have read. Compare evidence in the text to historical facts from the same place and time period to support your conclusions.	4	**Requires locating numerous pieces of specific evidence from multiple sources for comparison before drawing conclusions.**
9. Invent a new word. Include its definition, root, affix, part of speech, synonyms, antonyms, an example, a sentence using the word, and the context in which you believe the word would be understood.	2	**Requires making and applying word knowledge connections; requires creative, but is not strategic, because the final product is basically an invented word defined and used in a sentence.**
10. Compose an original poem using one of the forms or genres we have studied. Include an analysis of the poem's construction using appropriate terminology and domain-specific language.	3	**Requires deep analysis of one style/genre of poetry and applying it in an original composition.**
11. Read two or three short biographical sketches of authors who have written in a specific genre category. Illustrate or report on what elements they have in common.	2	**Locating information across sources using primarily explicit information (e.g., skimming for facts); focus is on compare-contrast; directions do not require drawing conclusions or deeper insights that need to be supported with reasoning or evidence.**
12. Select one of the Van Gogh paintings at https://www.vangoghmuseum.nl/en/collection. Create an implicit statement about what you see, such as describing the style or mood. Then use visual evidence to support your interpretations, such as how it portrays peacefulness, sadness, despair, or power.	3	**Requires deep analysis of one source, applying elements of art, principles or design, etc. Interpreting mood requires inferences based on supporting visual evidence.**

(continued)

A.1. Suggested Responses for Table 1.3, Analyzing the Intended DOK Levels of Learning or Assessment Tasks (*continued*)

Task Examples	Intended DOK Level?	What mental processing is called upon to complete the task?
13. Make a table showing the advantages and disadvantages of _____.	2	Compare-contrast mostly explicit information, even if facts are coming from multiple sources. Analysis is not specified in directions.
14. Two friends were arguing about the best seat in the movie theater. One of them had heard that it is best to sit so that the angle formed by the line of sight between the left and right sides of the screen is 30 degrees. John believes there is only one seat in the theater that meets this criterion. Amy argues there is more than one place where the viewing angle is also 30 degrees. Decide who is correct and provide supporting mathematical evidence.	3	Requires understanding one problem context to analyze it from two different perspectives; supporting evidence (calculations, measurements, diagrams, words) are required in presenting the solution.
15. Create a game that will teach your classmates about ________. Include important facts, concepts, and related images. Provide a set of directions with your game.	2	Most games tend to be fact-based and concept-based; they do not require much, if any, analysis. Directions summarize procedures used to play the game.
16. Create a model of one system of the human body. Label each organ/part of the body system describing how the parts of the system work together. Be prepared to answer questions about what might be the short- and longer-term result if a particular part malfunctions or there is an injury to the system.	3	Creating the visual display is DOK 1–2 (showing parts and relationships). Student must know one system in depth in order to respond to questions and possible results of malfunctioning, using supporting evidence.
17. Investigate how water pollution affects the fishing industry, and which states are most significantly impacted. Create a presentation to share your analysis of the impact of pollution on fishing in these states using specific examples.	3	Requires "looking up" specific information (e.g., retrieving facts from avariety of sources) in order to make connections, provide examples, explain cause-effect, and summarize information. Some analysis and planning are required to develop and deliver a presentation on a single topic—water pollution.

A.2. Where to Find Suggested Responses to Anticipation Guide (Activity 2.1), Pre-Post Self-Assessment: What is your current understanding of DOK?

D Disagree	A Agree	STEP 1: Do you agree/disagree (X) with each statement below? If you're not sure, go with your gut feeling right now.	STEP 2: Explain your thinking right now.	STEP 3: After completing the module, has your thinking changed or been confirmed? What sources/evidence help to explain your thinking now?
	X	1. All students can think deeply and engage in complex work.		**Misconception # 1**
X		2. DOK level is influenced by a student's grade level or completing tasks independently.		**Misconception # 1**
	X	3. Collaboration does *not* decrease the DOK level of a task.		**Misconception # 1**
X		4. Webb's DOK Framework is designed as a taxonomy, like Bloom's taxonomy.		**Misconception # 2**
X		5. Specific verbs for each DOK level can be used to plan lessons or write test questions.		**Misconception # 3**
X		6. DOK levels are influenced by the difficulty of a task, or the amount of time or effort required to complete it.		**Misconception # 4**
X		7. All DOK levels can be assessed with multiple-choice questions.		**Misconception # 5**
	X	8. Anyone, of any ability level, taking on a complex challenge can benefit from scaffolding.		**Misconception # 1**
X		9. Only higher-order verbs of Bloom's taxonomy (analyze, evaluate, create) lead to deep understanding.		**Misconception # 6**
	X	10. Completing multistep tasks or reading complex texts are *not* indicators of higher DOK levels.		**Misconception # 7**
X		11. DOK levels from 1 to 4 represent learning progressions.		**Misconception # 2**
X		12. Providing scaffolding for a task decreases complexity.		**Misconception # 1**

Hess Cognitive Rigor Matrices

Tools 1–8 can be downloaded at https://www.karin-hess.com/cognitive-rigor-and-dok

TOOL 1

HESS COGNITIVE RIGOR MATRIX | READING-LISTENING CRM

Integrating Depth-of-Knowledge Levels with Bloom's Cognitive Process Dimensions

Revised Bloom's Taxonomy	DOK Level 1 Recall and Reproduction	DOK Level 2 Skills and Concepts	DOK Level 3 Strategic Thinking or Reasoning	DOK Level 4 Extended Thinking
Remember Retrieve knowledge from long-term memory, recognize, recall, locate, identify	o Recall, recognize, or locate basic facts, terms, details, events, or ideas explicit in texts o Read words orally in connected text with fluency and accuracy	Use these Hess CRM curricular examples with most close reading or listening assignments or assessments in any content area.		
Understand Construct meaning, clarify, paraphrase, represent, translate, illustrate, give examples, classify, categorize, summarize, generalize, infer a logical conclusion, predict, compare–contrast, match like ideas, explain, construct models	o Identify or describe literary elements (characters, setting, sequence, etc.) o Select appropriate words when intended meaning or definition is clearly evident o Describe or explain who, what, where, when, or how o Define or describe facts, details, terms, principles o Write simple sentences	o Specify, explain, show relationships; explain why (e.g., cause–effect) o Give non examples or examples o Summarize results, concepts, ideas o Make basic inferences or logical predictions from data or texts o Identify main ideas or accurate generalizations of texts o Locate information to support explicit-implicit central ideas	o Explain, generalize, or connect ideas using supporting evidence (quote, example, text reference) o Identify or make inferences about explicit or implicit themes o Describe how word choice, point of view, or bias may affect the readers' interpretation of a text o Write multi paragraph composition for specific purpose, focus, voice, tone, and audience	o Explain how concepts or ideas specifically relate to other content domains (e.g., social, political, historical) or concepts o Develop generalizations of the results obtained or strategies used and apply them to new problem-based situations
Apply Carry out or use a procedure in a given situation; carry out (apply to a familiar task), or use (apply) to an unfamiliar task	o Use language structure (pre-, or suffix) or word relationships (synonym or antonym) to determine meaning of words o Apply rules or resources to edit spelling, grammar, punctuation, conventions, word use o Apply basic formats for documenting sources	o Use context to identify the meaning of words or phrases o Obtain and interpret information using text features o Develop a text that may be limited to one paragraph o Apply simple organizational structures (paragraph, sentence types) in writing	o Apply a concept in a new context o Revise final draft for meaning or progression of ideas o Apply internal consistency of text organization and structure to composing a full composition o Apply word choice, point of view, style to impact readers' or viewers' interpretation of a text	o Illustrate how multiple themes (historical, geographic, social, artistic, literary) may be interrelated o Select or devise an approach among many alternatives to research a novel problem
Analyze Break into constituent parts, determine how parts relate, differentiate between relevant-irrelevant, distinguish, focus, select, organize, outline, find coherence, deconstruct (e.g., for bias or point of view)	o Identify whether specific information is contained in graphic representations (e.g., map, chart, table, graph, T-chart, diagram) or text features (e.g., headings, subheadings, captions) o Decide which text structure is appropriate to audience and purpose	o Categorize or compare literary elements, terms, facts or details, events o Identify use of literary devices o Analyze format, organization, and internal text structure (signal words, transitions, semantic cues) of different texts o Distinguish: relevant-irrelevant information; fact or opinion o Identify characteristic text features; distinguish between texts, genres	o Analyze information within data sets or texts o Analyze interrelationships among concepts, issues, problems o Analyze or interpret author's craft (literary devices, viewpoint, or potential bias) to create or critique a text o Use reasoning, planning, and evidence to support inferences	o Analyze multiple sources of evidence, or multiple works by the same author, or across genres, time periods, themes o Analyze complex or abstract themes, perspectives, concepts o Gather, analyze, and organize multiple information sources o Analyze discourse styles
Evaluate Make judgments based on criteria, check, detect inconsistencies or fallacies, judge, critique	"UG"—unsubstantiated generalizations = stating an opinion without providing any support for it!		o Cite evidence and develop a logical argument for conjectures o Describe, compare, and contrast solution methods o Verify reasonableness of results o Justify or critique conclusions drawn	o Evaluate relevancy, accuracy, and completeness of information from multiple sources o Apply understanding in a novel way, provide argument or justification for the application
Create Reorganize elements into new patterns or structures, generate, hypothesize, design, plan, produce	o Brainstorm ideas, concepts, problems, or perspectives related to a topic, principle, or concept	o Generate conjectures or hypotheses based on observations or prior knowledge and experience	o Synthesize information within one source or text o Develop a complex model for a given situation o Develop an alternative solution	o Synthesize information across multiple sources or texts o Articulate a new voice, alternate theme, new knowledge or perspective

TOOL 2

HESS COGNITIVE RIGOR MATRIX | MATH-SCIENCE CRM

Integrating Depth-of-Knowledge Levels with Bloom's Cognitive Process Dimensions

Revised Bloom's Taxonomy	DOK Level 1 Recall and Reproduction	DOK Level 2 Skills and Concepts	DOK Level 3 Strategic Thinking or Reasoning	DOK Level 4 Extended Thinking
Remember Retrieve knowledge from long-term memory, recognize, recall, locate, identify	o Recall, observe, and recognize facts, principles, properties o Recall/ identify conversions among representations or numbers (e.g., customary and metric measures)	Use these Hess CRM curricular examples with most mathematics or science assignments or assessments.		
Understand Construct meaning, clarify, paraphrase, represent, translate, illustrate, give examples, classify, categorize, summarize, generalize, infer a logical conclusion, predict, compare–contrast, match like ideas, explain, construct models	o Evaluate an expression o Locate points on a grid or number on number line o Solve a one-step problem o Represent math relationships in words, pictures, or symbols o Read, write, compare decimals in scientific notation	o Specify and explain relationships (e.g., non examples or examples; cause-effect) o Make and record observations o Explain steps followed o Summarize results or concepts o Make basic inferences or logical predictions from data or observations o Use models or diagrams to represent or explain mathematical concepts o Make and explain estimates	o Use concepts to solve non routine problems o Explain, generalize, or connect ideas using supporting evidence o Make and justify conjectures o Explain thinking or reasoning when more than one solution or approach is possible o Explain phenomena in terms of concepts	o Relate mathematical or scientific concepts to other content areas, other domains, or other concepts o Develop generalizations of the results obtained and the strategies used (from investigation or readings) and apply them to new problem situations
Apply Carry out or use a procedure in a given situation; carry out (apply to a familiar task), or use (apply) to an unfamiliar task	o Follow simple procedures (recipe-type directions) o Calculate, measure, apply a rule (e.g., rounding) o Apply algorithm or formula (e.g., area, per meter) o Solve linear equations o Make conversions among representations or numbers, or within and between customary and metric measures	o Select a procedure according to criteria and perform it o Solve routine problem applying multiple concepts or decision points o Retrieve information from a table, graph, or figure and use it solve a problem requiring multiple steps o Translate between tables, graphs, words, and symbolic notations (e.g., graph data from a table) o Construct models given criteria	o Design investigation for a specific purpose or research question o Conduct a designed investigation o Use concepts to solve non routine problems o Use and show reasoning, planning, and evidence o Translate between problem and symbolic notation when not a direct translation	o Select or devise approach among many alternatives to solve a problem o Conduct a project that specifies a problem, identifies solution paths, solves the problem, and reports results
Analyze Break into constituent parts, determine how parts relate, differentiate between relevant-irrelevant, distinguish, focus, select, organize, outline, find coherence, deconstruct	o Retrieve information from a table or graph to answer a question o Identify whether specific information is contained in graphic representations (e.g., table, graph, T-chart, diagram) o Identify a pattern or trend	o Categorize, classify materials, data, figures based on characteristics o Organize or order data o Compare–contrast figures or data o Select appropriate graph and organize and display data o Interpret data from a simple graph o Extend a pattern	o Compare information within or across data sets or texts o Analyze and draw conclusions from data, citing evidence o Generalize a pattern o Interpret data from complex graph o Analyze similarities–differences between procedures or solutions	o Analyze multiple sources of evidence o Analyze complex or abstract themes o Gather, analyze, and evaluate information
Evaluate Make judgments based on criteria, check, detect inconsistencies or fallacies, judge, critique	"UG"—unsubstantiated generalizations = stating an opinion without providing any support for it!		o Cite evidence and develop a logical argument for concepts or solutions o Describe, compare, and contrast solution methods o Verify reasonableness of results	o Gather, analyze, and evaluate information to draw conclusions o Apply understanding in a novel way, provide argument or justification for the application
Create Reorganize elements into new patterns or structures, generate, hypothesize, design, plan, produce	o Brainstorm ideas, concepts, or perspectives related to a topic	o Generate conjectures or hypotheses based on observations or prior knowledge and experience	o Synthesize information within one data set, source, or text o Formulate an original problem given a situation o Develop a scientific/mathematical model for a complex situation	o Synthesize information across multiple sources or texts o Design a mathematical model to inform and solve a practical or abstract situation

TOOL 3

HESS COGNITIVE RIGOR MATRIX | WRITING-SPEAKING CRM

Integrating Depth-of-Knowledge Levels with Bloom's Cognitive Process Dimensions

Revised Bloom's Taxonomy	DOK Level 1 Recall and Reproduction	DOK Level 2 Skills and Concepts	DOK Level 3 Strategic Thinking or Reasoning	DOK Level 4 Extended Thinking
Remember Retrieve knowledge from long-term memory, recognize, recall, locate, identify	o Complete short answer questions with facts, details, terms, principles, etc. (e.g., label parts of diagram)	Use these Hess CRM curricular examples with most writing and oral communication assignments or assessments in any content area.		
Understand Construct meaning, clarify, paraphrase, represent, translate, illustrate, give examples, classify, categorize, summarize, generalize, infer a logical conclusion, predict, compare–contrast, match like ideas, explain, construct models	o Describe or define facts, details, terms, principles, etc. o Select appropriate word or phrase to use when intended meaning or definition is clearly evident o Write simple complete sentences o Add an appropriate caption to a photo or illustration o Write "fact statements" on a topic (e.g., spiders build webs)	o Specify, explain, show relationships; explain why, cause–effect o Provide and explain non examples and examples o Take notes; organize ideas or data (e.g., relevance, trends, perspectives) o Summarize results, key concepts, ideas o Explain central ideas or accurate generalizations of texts or topics o Describe steps in a process (e.g., science procedure, how to and why control variables)	o Write a multi paragraph composition for specific purpose, focus, voice, tone, and audience o Develop and explain opposing perspectives or connect ideas, principles, or concepts using supporting evidence (quote, example, text reference, etc.) o Develop arguments of fact (e.g., Are these criticisms supported by the historical facts? Is this claim or equation true?)	o Use multiple sources to elaborate on how concepts or ideas specifically draw from other content domains or differing concepts (e.g., research paper, arguments of policy—should this law be passed? What will be the impact of this change?) o Develop generalizations about the results obtained or strategies used and apply them to a new problem or contextual scenario
Apply Carry out or use a procedure in a given situation; carry out (apply to a familiar task), or use (apply) to an unfamiliar task	o Apply rules or use resources to edit specific spelling, grammar, punctuation, conventions, or word use o Apply basic formats for documenting sources	o Use context to identify or infer the intended meaning of words or phrases o Obtain, interpret, and explain information using text features (table, diagram, etc.) o Develop a (brief) text that may be limited to one paragraph, précis o Apply basic organizational structures (paragraph, sentence types, topic sentence, introduction, etc.) in writing	o Revise final draft for meaning, progression of ideas, or logic chain o Apply internal consistency of text organization and structure to a full composition or oral communication o Apply a concept in a new context o Apply word choice, point of view, style, rhetorical devices to impact readers' interpretation of a text	o Select or devise an approach among many alternatives to research and present a novel problem or issue o Illustrate how multiple themes (historical, geographic, social) may be interrelated within a text or topic
Analyze Break into constituent parts, determine how parts relate, differentiate between relevant-irrelevant, distinguish, focus, select, organize, outline, find coherence, deconstruct (e.g., for bias or point of view)	o Decide which text structure is appropriate to audience and purpose (e.g., compare–contrast, proposition–support) o Determine appropriate, relevant key words for conducting an Internet search or researching a topic	o Compare–contrast perspectives, events, characters, etc. o Analyze–revise format, organization, and internal text structure (signal words, transitions, semantic cues) of different print and non print texts o Distinguish: relevant–irrelevant information; fact–opinion (e.g., What are the characteristics of a hero's journey?) o Locate evidence that supports a perspective–differing perspectives	o Analyze interrelationships among concepts, issues, and problems in a text o Analyze impact or use of author's craft (literary devices, viewpoint, dialogue) in a single text o Use reasoning and evidence to generate criteria for making and supporting an argument of judgment (Was FDR a great president? Who was the greatest ball player?) o Support conclusions with evidence	o Analyze multiple sources of evidence, or multiple works by the same author, or across genres, or time periods o Analyze complex or abstract themes, perspectives, concepts o Gather, analyze, and organize multiple information sources o Compare and contrast conflicting judgments or policies (e.g., Supreme Court decisions)
Evaluate Make judgments based on criteria, check, detect inconsistencies or fallacies, judge, critique	"UG"—unsubstantiated generalizations = stating an opinion without providing any support for it!		o Evaluate validity and relevance of evidence used to develop an argument or support a perspective o Describe, compare, and contrast solution methods o Verify or critique the accuracy, logic, and reasonableness of stated conclusions or assumptions	o Evaluate relevancy, accuracy, and completeness of information across multiple sources o Apply understanding in a novel way, provide argument or justification for the application o Critique the historical impact (policy, writings, discoveries, etc.)
Create Reorganize elements into new patterns or structures, generate, hypothesize, design, plan, produce	o Brainstorm facts, ideas, concepts, problems, or perspectives related to a topic, text, idea, issue, or concept	o Generate conjectures, hypotheses , or predictions based on facts, observations, evidence/observations, or prior knowledge and experience o Generate believable "grounds" (reasons) for an opinion-argument	o Develop a complex model for a given situation or problem o Develop an alternative solution or perspective to one proposed (e.g., debate)	o Synthesize information across multiple sources or texts in order to articulate a new voice, alternate theme, new knowledge or nuanced perspective

TOOL 4

HESS COGNITIVE RIGOR MATRIX | SOCIAL STUDIES-HUMANITIES CRM

Integrating Depth-of-Knowledge Levels with Bloom's Cognitive Process Dimensions

Revised Bloom's Taxonomy	DOK Level 1 Recall and Reproduction	DOK Level 2 Skills and Concepts	DOK Level 3 Strategic Thinking or Reasoning	DOK Level 4 Extended Thinking
Remember Retrieve knowledge from long-term memory, recognize, recall, locate, identify	o Recall or locate key facts dates, terms, details, events, or ideas explicit in texts	Use these Hess CRM curricular examples with most assignments, assessments, or inquiry activities in social studies, history, civics, geography, economics, or humanities.		
Understand Construct meaning, clarify, paraphrase, represent, translate, illustrate, give examples, classify, categorize, summarize, generalize, infer a logical conclusion, predict, observe, compare-contrast, match like ideas, explain, construct models	o Select appropriate words or terms when intended meaning is clearly evident o Describe or explain who, what, where, when, or how o Define facts, details, terms, principles o Locate or identify symbols that represent . . . o Raise related questions for possible investigation	o Specify, explain, illustrate relationships; explain why (e.g., cause–effect) o Provide and explain non examples and examples o Summarize results, concepts, main ideas, generalizations o Make basic inferences or logical predictions (using data or text) o Locate relevant information to support explicit-implicit central ideas	o Explain, generalize, or connect ideas using supporting evidence (quote, example, text reference, data) o Support inferences about explicit or implicit themes o Describe how word choice, point of view, or bias may affect the reader or viewer interpretation o Write multi-paragraph composition or essay for specific purpose, focus, voice, tone, and audience	o Explain how concepts or ideas specifically relate to other content domains or concepts (social, political, historical, cultural) o Apply generalizations to new problem-based situations o Use multiple sources to elaborate on how concepts or ideas specifically draw from other content domains or differing concepts (e.g., research paper, arguments of policy: Should this law be passed? What will be the impact of this change?)
Apply Carry out or use a procedure in a given situation; carry out (apply to a familiar task), or use (transfer) to an unfamiliar or non routine task	o Apply basic formats for documenting sources o Apply use of reference materials and tools for gathering information (e.g., key word searches)	o Use context to identify the meaning of words or phrases o Interpret information using text features (diagrams, data tables, captions, etc.) o Apply simple organizational structures (paragraph outline)	o Investigate to determine how an historical, cultural or political context may be the source of an underlying theme, central idea, or unresolved issue or crisis	o Integrate or juxtapose multiple (historical, cultural) contexts drawn from source materials (e.g., literature, music, historical events, media) with intent to develop a complex or multimedia product and personal viewpoint
Analyze Break into constituent parts, determine how parts relate, differentiate between relevant-irrelevant, distinguish, focus, select, organize, outline, find coherence, deconstruct (e.g., for bias, point of view, approach/strategy used)	o Identify causes or effects o Describe processes or tools used to research ideas, artifacts, or images reflecting history, culture, tradition, etc. o Identify ways symbols and metaphors are used to represent universal ideas o Identify specific information given in graphics (e.g., map, T-chart, diagram) or text features (e.g., heading, subheading, captions)	o Compare similarities or differences in processes, methods, styles due to influences of time period, politics or culture o Distinguish relevant–irrelevant information, fact or opinion; primary from a secondary source o Draw inferences about social, historical, cultural contexts portrayed in (literature, arts, film, political cartoons, primary sources) o Explain, categorize events or ideas in the evolution of ______ across time periods	o Analyze information within data sets or a text (e.g., interrelationships among concepts, issues, problems) o Analyze an author's viewpoint or potential bias (e.g., political cartoon) o Use reasoning, planning, and evidence to support or refute inferences in policy or speech o Use reasoning and evidence to generate criteria for making and supporting an 'argument of judgment' (e.g., Was FDR a great president? Is this a fair law?)	o Analyze multiple sources of evidence across time periods, themes, issues o Analyze diverse, complex or abstract perspectives o Gather, analyze, and organize information from multiple sources o Analyze discourse styles or bias in speeches, legal briefs, etc. across time or authors o Compare and contrast conflicting judgments or policies (e.g., Supreme Court decisions)
Evaluate Make judgments based on criteria, check, detect inconsistencies or fallacies, judge, critique	"UG"—unsubstantiated generalizations = stating an opinion without providing any support for it!		o Develop a logical argument for conjectures, citing evidence o Verify reasonableness of results of others o Critique conclusions drawn, evidence used, credibility of sources	o Evaluate relevancy, accuracy, and completeness of information using multiple sources o Apply understanding in a novel way, provide argument or justification for the application o Critique the historical impact on policy, writings, advances
Create Reorganize elements into new patterns,structures, or schemas, generate, hypothesize, design, plan, producee	o Brainstorm ideas, concepts, problems, or perspectives related to a topic , principle, or concept	o Generate testable conjectures or hypotheses based on observations, prior knowledge, and/or artifacts	o Synthesize information within one source or text o Develop a complex model or symbol for given issue o Develop and support an alternative solution	o Synthesize information across multiple sources or texts o Articulate a new voice, alternate theme, new knowledge or new perspective o Create historical fiction drawing on sources

TOOL 5

HESS COGNITIVE RIGOR MATRIX | FINE ARTS CRM

Integrating Depth-of-Knowledge Levels with Artistic Practices

Artistic Practice	**DOK Level 1** **Recall and Reproduction** Having the knowledge required; do not need to "figure it out"	**DOK Level 2** **Connect or Apply Skills and Concepts** Making connections among skills or concepts or decisions (e.g., about approach, tools)	**DOK Level 3** **Strategic Thinking or Abstract Reasoning** Complex and Abstract; Exploring multiple solution paths; Justifying *with evidence*	**DOK Level 4** **Extended Thinking** Relating or developing complex ideas using multi sources *and evidence*
Perceiving, Performing, and Responding	o Identify or describe ways art represents what people see, hear, feel, believe o Recall or describe a variety of instruments, forms, symbols, rhythms, conventions of music o Describe how artists or dancers might represent . . . o Identify or describe narrative conventions depicted in the arts	o Show relationships between (dance, music, film, etc.) and other arts forms o Make observations or compare similarities or differences: styles, forms, techniques, etc. o Explain possible reasons for selecting tools, medium, elements, principles, images, etc. o Select a familiar artistic work to perform o Explain the artist's central message	o Analyze or find evidence of how a combination of elements or principles are used to achieve a desired effect or theme o Analyze narrative art work, using supporting evidence to interpret setting, characters, action, conflict, etc. o Develop personal response to or interpretation of a work of art	o Analyze more than one performance or product (same composer, time period, theme, etc.) drawing from multiple source materials for the analyses (e.g., different treatments of same theme) o Perform an "old" idea in a new way
Historical, Social, and Cultural Contexts	o Describe processes used by artists to select or create ideas, images that reflect history, culture, tradition, etc. o Identify ways symbols and metaphors are used to represent universal ideas o Locate symbols that represent… o Identify or describe characteristics and origins of dance, art, or music genres	o Draw inferences about social, historical, or cultural contexts portrayed in art, music, dance, theatre, or film o Explain or compare how different art forms communicate culture, time period, issues o Compare similarities or differences in processes, methods, styles due to influences of time period, politics, or culture o Explain or trace the evolution of arts forms across time periods	o Analyze how historical or cultural context is applied to develop theme in a performance or product o Plan artworks based on historical, social, political, or cultural theme, concept, or representative style o Apply problem solving strategies used among the arts, humanities, and sciences to solve visual "problems"	o Integrate or juxtapose *multiple (historical, cultural) contexts drawn from source materials* (e.g., literature, music, historical events, media) with intent to develop a complex or multifaceted performance or product and personal viewpoint
Creative Expression, Exploration, and Production	o Explore ideas and techniques by manipulating media, materials, tools for different effects (e.g., how color, rhythm, or camera angles create various moods) o Demonstrate a variety of movements, methods, techniques o Locate or compile examples illustrating different approaches (e.g., camera angles; use of white space)	o Select or use tools for specific artistic purposes o Develop a study of ________ by combining elements, aesthetic principles, and/or forms, etc. o Use or apply choreographic forms to communicate ideas, feelings, concepts o Improvise simple rhythmic variations o Create examples or models that represent the same topic, concept, idea, etc.	o Combine elements of (dance, art, music) to create ________ that conveys an intended point of view or specific idea, mood, or theme o Create or compose for a specific purpose, using appropriate processes, tools, techniques o Create narrative art work depicting setting, characters, action, conflict, etc. o Research a given style and develop personal interpretation of it	o Apply *multiple sets of criteria* to develop and present a complex or multifaceted performance or product (e.g., consistent application of awareness of space, physical discipline, concentration, and projection from rehearsals to performance; development of portfolio showing evolution of ideas or personal style)
Aesthetics, Criticism, and Reflection	o Recognize or describe choreographic forms, elements of art or music, principles of design, etc. when presented in isolation o Describe criteria used for executing technical or artistic quality	o Explain ways in which artistic choices (choreographic forms, etc.) might affect performance or audience response o Critique examples and non-examples of a given technique, style, etc.	o Defend the selection of criteria and evidence used to critique the quality or develop a performance or product (e.g., compose a melody, perform improvisation, direct a scene, solve a visual "problem")	o Formulate or use *multiple sets of criteria* and evidence to critique a complex or multi faceted performance or final product o Compile and defend exemplars chosen to depict a theme or style

TOOL 6

HESS COGNITIVE RIGOR MATRIX | HEALTH AND PHYSICAL EDUCATION CRM

Porter 's Cognitive Demand Catego-ries	DOK Level 1 **Recall and Reproduction** Having the knowledge required; do not need to "figure it out"	DOK Level 2 **Connect or Apply Skills and Concepts** Making connections among skills or concepts or decisions (e.g., about approach, tools)	DOK Level 3 **Strategic Thinking or Abstract Reasoning** Complex and Abstract; Exploring multiple solution paths; Justifying *with evidence*	DOK Level 4 **Extended Thinking** Relating or developing complex ideas using multi sources *and evidence*
Memorize	o Recall or identify basic facts, terms, definitions, skills, rules, principles, concepts, symbols o Acquire new terms, vocabulary, etc.	Use these Hess CRM Curricular Examples with most assignments, assessments, or learning activities for Health and Physical Education. See also the Hess CRM for Fine Arts with examples for dance.		
Communicate Understanding	o Define terms, principles, concepts o Describe how to perform a routine skill or task o Use words, visuals, or symbols to represent basic ideas, movements, procedures, etc.	o Explain concepts: show or predict relationships (if-then, cause-effect); provide examples and non examples o Observe and interpret teacher or student demonstrations o Summarize a concept, series of events, movements, or a result	o Use evidence (data, examples, source, observations) to justify an interpretation of a result or performance o Locate or reproduce supporting evidence for results of effectiveness of a plan (e.g., exercise or diet routine) o Create a personal plan when given criteria	o Share results of comparing different plans (e.g., compare exercise or diet routines) using data and evidence from multiple sources or data sets o Explain how a concept relates across content domains or to "big ideas" (e.g., systems, patterns)
Perform Procedures	o Safely demonstrate or use appropriate tools or equipment o Execute or repeat basic skills or procedures (e.g., follow step-by-step directions or pattern) o Demonstrate a basic skill sequence, movement pattern, etc., with smooth transitions	o Make observations; collect and record data and observations (e.g., health diary, skills progress) o Select and use appropriate tool or equipment for a given task o Complete routine tasks in a fitness assessment	o Plan, execute, and evaluate multi step procedures (a dance routine, football play, rules of a new game, etc.) o Test effects and trends of using different activities by observing and collecting data (e.g., exercise or diet routines) o Select and plan how to use a combination of movements to achieve a desired effect	o Design and conduct a performance (e.g., exercise or dance routine) using multiple sources or resources, and or given constraints (e.g., use of space) o Test effects of different variables on performance (e.g., applied to a new situation)
Apply Concepts/ Make Connections	o Apply rules or score-keeping of a game or simple routine o Apply appropriate content-specific vocabulary or terms to tasks o Brainstorm ideas, problems, or perspectives related to a situation, scenario, or observation	o Create an infographic or visual to show connections or to summarize key ideas (e.g., cause-effect, heart rate-activity type, warm up-cool down, healthy or unhealthy) o Explain connections among concepts or skills in a given context (e.g., movement or open space concepts, health benefits)	o Revise a plan (self, peer) based on feedback and evidence o Use concepts to explain phenomena or research or medical advances (e.g., use of steroids, drugs, food choices) o Investigate how an event or advancement led to a new perspective or outcome	o Apply and adapt information and concepts to real-world situations o Integrate ideas from multiple sources to extend an idea or solve a problem with an alternative solution o Trace the evolution of (game, drug, etc.) from past to present, citing sources used
Analyze Information	o Identify, describe, match, or name parts in a diagram or visual (e.g., muscle groups or skeletal system) or patterns o Determine which skill, rule, or principle applies to a given situation o Record performance data	o Compare-contrast routines, skill sets, or qualities (e.g., use T-chart, graphic organizer for locomotor-non locomotor) o Generate questions and make predictions based on observations or information o Classify types of . . . (movements, sports, symptoms, examples, etc.)	o Analyze data in order to recognize patterns or draw conclusions based on evidence (e.g., batting averages, areas needing remediation) o Identify faulty arguments, strategies, or misrepresentations of data or media message o Defend the selection of criteria used to critique or develop a performance or product	o Research a topic in-depth, evaluating relevancy, accuracy, and completeness of information from multiple sources or perspectives o Analyze evidence and recommend the most effective course of action for intended purpose (e.g., food, fitness)

TOOL 7

HESS COGNITIVE RIGOR MATRIX | WORLD LANGUAGES CRM

Integrating Depth-of-Knowledge Levels with World Language Practices and Modes of Communication

World Language Practices and Modes of Communication	**DOK Level 1** **Recall and Reproduction** Having the knowledge required; do not need to "figure it out""	**DOK Level 2** **Skills and Concepts** Making connections among skills or concepts or decisions (e.g., about approach, tools)	**DOK Level 3** **Strategic Thinking or Reasoning** Complex and Abstract; Exploring multiple solution paths; Justifying *with evidence*	**DOK Level 4** **Extended Thinking** Relating or developing complex ideas using multi sources *and evidence*
Memorize and Recall	o Reproduce, recall, or repeat vocabulary, grammar rules, facts, definitions, dictated statements, etc. o Describe cultural conventions o Recite in sequence (e.g., alphabet, counting, songs, rhymes)	Use these World Language CRM curricular examples for designing most language and communication assignments or assessment tasks.		
Interpersonal Communication Understand, Perceive, and Respond	o Understand simple, familiar messages in social settings o Identify everyday objects o Follow simple oral directions or written procedures (recipe, etc.) o Convey simple messages, express feelings (e.g., I'm sad because...) o Ask or answer literal questions after reading, listening, or viewing	o Explain how or why alternative responses may be correct (where do you live?) for different situations o Carry on a short conversation using familiar vocabulary and grammar o Paraphrase, summarize, or retell what was said, read, viewed (with cues) o Make logical predictions (e.g., what might happen next . . .); describe event	o Prepare for an interview or develop survey on topic of interest anticipating audience questions or possible responses o Initiate and extend a conversation about an unfamiliar topic, appropriately using language mechanics or tense throughout o Create a theme-based photo essay o Justify interpretation of purpose or tone (in media message, photo essay, etc.)	o Carry on an extended conversation responding appropriately to multiple speakers (e.g., using multiple tenses, asking and answering, elaborating on ideas, raising questions) o Deepen knowledge of a topic using multiple (oral, visual, textual) sources for an informational communication (e.g., "by the numbers" infographic)
Interpret and Apply	o Match vocabulary (e.g., picture–word; synonyms); locate details o Apply a spelling or grammar rule (e.g., conjugate a verb, make plural) o Use resources to translate literally o Use nouns or verbs in familiar contexts	o Infer and explain meaning using context, cognates, or structure in a familiar situation o Translate to identify use of non-literal, figurative, or idiomatic language o Sequence events for given text or visual	o Explain inferences or colloquial expressions using supporting evidence o Interpret symbolic or abstract meaning (from music, video, reading, art, etc.) o Interpret idiomatic or figurative language in context (poem, song lyric, media, etc.)	o Make and justify conclusions based on 2+ ads for the same product or two political cartoons about the same event or person o Write, draw, or perform in the style of a known author/artist/cartoonist
Compare, Analyze, Critique or Evaluate, and Reflect	o Edit a sentence or phrase o Select appropriate word or phrase for intended meaning o Answer what, when, and where questions using a source (map, calendar, schedule, visual, photo) o Connect words or phrases between languages (origins, meanings, etc.)	o Categorize or compare (objects, foods, tools, people, etc.) using oral, physical, or textual stimuli o Self-correct when speaking or reading o Evaluate message or cultural nuances (e.g., gestures, language) using listening and observational skills	o Evaluate and correct inaccuracy of a message - print or non-print text (e.g., facts, sequence, cultural nuances) o Support an opinion, argument, or disagreement with evidence, reasoning o Determine if source can or cannot answer specific questions and why (e.g., websites)	o Critique authentic literature, arts, or historical events from multiple sources: authors, perspectives, or time periods o Evaluate relevancy, accuracy, and completeness of information o Keep a journal and use it to reflect on or evaluate personal progress
Presentational Communication Produce or Create	o Represent vocabulary or common phrases in pictures, symbols, visuals, gestures, pantomime o Brainstorm related words, ideas, images, possible responses o Label information on a diagram, map, visual o Tell or select phrases as thumbnail sketch for a narrative text or story line	o Perform a memorized dialog o Choose which tense to use in a less familiar context o Create an ABC book connecting entries by central or organizing topic (e.g., animals, foods) o Create text messages or description (narration/voice over) for a visual stimuli or "muted" video scene o Make or label a timeline of key events	o Develop a vocabulary-based game to teach about geography, culture, etc. o Develop a new scene or ending, consistent with the original text o Create or perform a dialog based on visual stimuli or a current or cultural event (integrating academic vocabulary) o Co-plan website or event highlighting target culture (foods, traditions, places to visit)	o Produce an 'old' idea in a new way (e.g., multimedia, podcast) o Integrate ideas from several sources o Research a topic with evidence pro-con for debate, essay, or cartoon o Research and present performance or presentation using multiple sources o Design a theme-based café, including the menu, location, décor and develop an ad for targeted clientele

TOOL 8

HESS COGNITIVE RIGOR MATRIX | CAREER AND TECHNICAL EDUCATION (CTE) CRM

Revised Bloom's Taxonomy	DOK Level 1 Recall and Reproduction	DOK Level 2 Skills and Concepts	DOK Level 3 Strategic Thinking or Reasoning	DOK Level 4 Extended Thinking
Remember Memorize, recognize, recall, locate, identify	o Recall or locate key facts, terms, details, procedures (e.g., explicit in a technical manual)	Use these Hess CRM curricular examples with most assignments, assessments, or inquiry activities for Career and Technical Education		
Understand Construct meaning, clarify, paraphrase, represent, translate, illustrate, give examples, summarize, generalize, infer a logical conclusion, predict, observe, match like ideas, explain, construct models	o Select correct terms or graphics for intended meaning o Describe or explain who, what, where, when, or how o Define terms, principles, concepts o Represent relationships with words, diagrams, symbols o Solve routine problems	o Specify and explain relationships (e.g., non-examples/examples; cause-effect; if-then) o Summarize procedures, results, concepts, key ideas (paragraph) o Make and explain estimates, basic inferences, or predictions o Use models to explain concepts o Make and record observations	o Explain, generalize, or connect ideas using supporting evidence (quote, example, text reference, data); o Justify your interpretation when more than one is plausible o Explain how a concept can be used to solve a non routine problem o Develop a multi paragraph manual or infographic for specific purpose or focus	o Use multiple sources to outline varying perspectives on a problem or issue o Explain how a concept relates across content domains or to 'big Ideas' (e.g., patterns in the human or designed world; structure–function) o Apply generalizations from one investigation to new problem-based situations, using evidence or data
Apply Carry out or use a procedure in a given situation; carry out (apply to a familiar task), or use (transfer) to an unfamiliar or non routine task	o Apply basic formulas, algorithms, conversion rules o Calculate; measure o Use reference materials and tools to gather information o Demo safe procedures	o Select and use appropriate tool or procedure for specified task o Use context to identify the meaning of terms or phrases o Interpret information using diagrams, data tables, etc.	o Build or revise a plan for investigation using (new) evidence or data o Use and show reasoning, planning, and evidence to support conclusions or to identify design flaws o Conduct a designed investigation	o Draw from source materials with intent to develop a complex or multimedia product with personal viewpoint o Conduct a project that specifies a problem, identifies solution paths, tests the solution, and reports results
Analyze Break into constituent parts, determine how parts relate, compare-contrast, differentiate between relevant–irrelevant, distinguish, focus, select, organize, outline, find coherence, deconstruct (e.g., for potential bias, point of view, technique or strategy used)	o Identify trend, pattern, possible cause, or effect o Describe processes or tools used to research ideas o Identify ways symbols or metaphors are used to represent universal ideas o Retrieve data to answer a question (e.g., diagram, graph)	o Compare similarities or differences or draw inferences about __________ due to influences of __________ o Distinguish relevant-irrelevant information; fact/opinion; primary from a secondary source o Extend a pattern o Organize and represent data o Categorize materials, data, etc., based on characteristics	o Interpret information from a complex graph or model (e.g., interrelationships among variables, concepts) o Use reasoning, planning, and evidence to support or refute inferences or results stated o Use reasoning and evidence to generate criteria for making and supporting an argument o Generalize and support a pattern/trend	o Analyze multiple sources of evidence (e.g., compare–contrast various plans, solution methods) o Analyze and compare diverse, complex, or abstract perspectives, models, etc. o Gather, organize, and analyze information from multiple sources to answer a research question
Evaluate Make judgments based on specified criteria, detect inconsistencies, flaws, or fallacies, judge, critique	"UG"—unsubstantiated generalizations = stating an opinion without providing any support for it		o Develop a logical argument for conjectures, citing evidence o Verify reasonableness of results or conjectures (e.g., of others) o Critique conclusions drawn or evidence used or credibility of sources	o Evaluate relevancy, accuracy, and completeness of sources used o Apply understanding in a novel way, provide argument or justification for the application o Critique the historical impact of __________ on __________.
Create Reorganize into new patterns or schemas, design, plan, produce	o Brainstorm ideas, concepts, problems, or perspectives related to a given scenario, observation, question posed	o Generate testable conjectures or hypotheses based on observations, prior knowledge, and/or artifacts	o Develop a complex model for given concept and justify reasoning o Develop an alternative solution and justify reasoning	o Synthesize information across multiple models, sources, or texts o Articulate new knowledge or new perspective

APPENDIX C

DOK Planning Tools

Interactive versions of Tools 9–13 can be downloaded at https://www.karin-hess.com/formative-and-performance-assessments

TOOL 9

TASK QUALITY VALIDATION PROTOCOL:

Purpose, Alignment, Engagement, & Fairness | Use for Assessment *Development* or *Analysis of Performance Tasks*

Title of Assessment/Task: Gr Level/Dept/Course/Subject:

Author(s): or Reviewer(s):

How will the assessment results be used?

(e.g., screening for placement; diagnostic to inform instruction or to provide targeted additional support; formative or interim for progress monitoring; summative for grading/report card; or other?)

Analyze and discuss each of the assessment components. Check box if there is evidence of each indicator of high-quality assessment listed. Then add any additional notes.

Clarity & Focus

☐ 1. Addresses an **essential issue, big idea, or key concept or skill** of the unit/course/discipline:

☐ 2. Directions/prompts clearly indicate what the student is being asked to do/produce:

☐ 3. If parts are completed within a group: Specifies what will be assessed **individually** (e.g., projects, multimedia presentations)

☐ 4. **Assesses what is intended to be assessed** – will elicit what the student knows and can do related to the chosen standards and benchmarks. **Any scaffolding** provided (e.g., task broken into smaller steps; graphic organizer to pre-plan) does not change what is actually being assessed.

☐ 5. Is clearly linked to **ongoing instruction/opportunity to learn** (e.g., assessed within or at the end of a unit of study/course)

Clarity & Focus Notes

Content Alignment: Academic or Personal Competencies

☐ 6. Items/tasks are clearly **aligned with specific competencies/essential skills/concepts** (or intended parts or competenciess)

☐ 7. Appropriate **rubric(s) or scoring guide(s)** assess all intended parts of competencies assessed. Scoring guides are useful in determining what the student knows/does not know, not simply yield a score. (E.g., what does a score of 25 really mean? What additional or next steps in instruction does the student need? Are some rubric criteria 'weighted' reflecting greater instructional emphasis for this time of year?)

☐ 8. **Exemplars/anchor papers** illustrate expectations aligned to competencies at proficient level and performance levels above / below proficient. **Qualitative distinctions between performance levels are evident.**

Content Alignment Notes

continued...

TOOL 9

TASK QUALITY VALIDATION PROTOCOL:

Purpose, Alignment, Engagement, & Fairness | Use for Assessment *Development* or *Analysis of Performance Tasks*

Rigor Alignment/Cognitive Demand

☐ 9. Identify Depth-of-Knowledge/ DOK levels assessed/emphasized (e.g., number of score points given, weighting in the rubric). For example, an essay would mostly assess DOK 3 (full multi-paragraph composition), but also have some DOK 2 items/parts (text organization, structure) and DOK 1 (grammar, conventions) also assessed. You would check "most of the test/task" for DOK 3 and "some of the test/task" for DOK 2 and DOK 1. (See Hess Cognitive Rigor Matrix /CRM Tools for content-specific descriptors of each DOK level.)

DOK 1: Students recall/locate/reproduce: words, terms, facts; basic application of rules, procedures, which may be routine and multi-step

(☐ most of test/task ☐ some of the test/task ☐ none of the test/task)

DOK 2: Students apply level 1 within the ability to paraphrase, summarize, interpret, infer, classify, organize, compare; determine fact from fiction; solve, as in routine word problems; determine meanings in context. There is a correct answer, but may involve multiple concepts/decision points.

(☐ most of test/task ☐ some of the test/task ☐ none of the test/task)

DOK 3: Students must support their thinking by citing evidence (e.g., text, data, calculations, models). Students are asked to go beyond the text/data collection to analyze, generalize, or connect to bigger ideas. Requires 'uncovering' and interpreting less explicit knowledge. Items may require abstract reasoning, alternate approaches, inferences that connect information, application of prior knowledge or text support for an analytical judgments.

(☐ most of test/task ☐ some of the test/task ☐ none of the test/task)

DOK 4: Students use deeper knowledge of content, and evidence of complex reasoning, planning, and developing new ideas/insights/products **from multiple sources**. Usually applies to an extended task or project. Examples: evaluate works by the same author; critique an issue across time periods or research topic/issue from different perspectives; longer science/math/arts investigations or research projects involving all phases of design, testing, and refining.

(☐ most of test/task ☐ some of the test/task ☐ none of the test/task)

☐ 10. Has alignment with the **intended rigor** of the competency (or parts/combinations of the essential skills/concepts). Scaffolding does not significantly reduce cognitive demand.

Rigor Alignment Notes

Student Engagement

☐ 11. The situation/scenario or application is **authentic.** Reflects a meaningful, real-world problem, issue, or theme worth exploring.

☐ 12. Provides for student ownership, **choice, and/or decision-making**; requires the student to be actively engaged in solution finding.

☐ 13. Is administered after students have had adequate time to learn, practice, and expand their understanding of skills/concepts assessed.

Student Engagement Notes

continued...

TOOL 9

TASK QUALITY VALIDATION PROTOCOL:

Purpose, Alignment, Engagement, & Fairness | Use for Assessment *Development* or *Analysis of Performance Tasks*

Fairness: Universal Access & Design Features

- ☐ 14. **Is fair and unbiased in language and design.**
  - ☐ Material is familiar to students from identifiable cultural, gender, linguistic, and other groups
  - ☐ The task stimulus /prompt and materials (context/texts used) are free of stereotypes
  - ☐ All students (e.g., all ability levels) are on a level playing field and have had opportunity to learn
  - ☐ All students have access to necessary resources (e.g. Internet, calculators, spellcheck, etc.)
  - ☐ Assessment conditions are the same for all students or flexible enough not to change what's actually being assessed (e.g., reading a passage aloud may be fine for interpreting overall meaning, but not for assessing ability to decode words)
  - ☐ The task can be reasonably completed under the specified conditions; extended time is allowable
  - ☐ The rubric or scoring guide allows for different response modes (oral, written, etc.)
- ☐ 15. **Adheres to the principles of Universal Design for Learning (UDL)**
  - ☐ Instructions are free of excessive wordiness or irrelevant (unnecessary) information
  - ☐ Instructions are free of unusual words (unusual spellings or unfamiliar word use) that the student may not understand or have been exposed to
  - ☐ Low frequency words (words not used in other content areas, such as technical terms) are only used when explicitly needed or when the assessment is explicitly testing understanding of terms
  - ☐ Instructions are free of ambiguous words
  - ☐ Irregularly spelled words have been avoided whenever possible
  - ☐ There are no proper names that students may not understand (e.g., students have never seen them before in instruction)
  - ☐ Multiple words, symbols, or pronouns, intended to mean the same thing are NOT used in the same sentence or stimulus/prompt (e.g., inches and the symbol " for inches; phrases such as: the boys, they, the friends)
  - ☐ The format/layout conveys the focus of the expected tasks and products and allows adequate space for responding
  - ☐ The format clearly indicates what the actual questions to answer or prompts are (e.g., each question/prompt is clearly separated from the introductory stimulus/problem context)
  - ☐ Questions/prompts are consistently marked with graphic or visual cues (bullets, numbers, in a text box, etc.)
  - ☐ The test format (spacing, presentation, etc.) is familiar, consistent, and predictable as to what students will be expected to do
- ☐ 16. **Allows for accommodations for students with IEPs/504 Plans.**
  - ☐ **Presentation**—Students may access information in ways that do not require them to visually read standard print (auditory, multi-sensory, tactile, and visual).
  - ☐ **Response**—Students may complete activities in different ways or use some type of assistive device or organizer to assist them in responding.
  - ☐ **Setting**—Location in which a test is given or the conditions of the assessment setting are flexible.
  - ☐ **Timing/ Scheduling**—The length of time to complete an assessment may be increased and/or the way the time is organized may be changed.

Fairness: Universal Access & Design Notes

TOOL 10

ANALYZING FORMATIVE ASSESSMENTS STRATEGIC PLANNING TOOL

What (thinking or learning) will this formative assessment uncover?

List formative assessment task(s) or probing question(s):

Content Standard(s) Assessed:

Intended Depth-of-Knowledge (DOK) Level(s): ☐ DOK 1 ☐ DOK 2 ☐ DOK 3 ☐ DOK 4

LEARNING TARGET:

Expected Understandings		Possible Misunderstandings	
Concepts and Reasoning	**Skills and Procedures**	**Common Errors**	**Overgeneralizations**
If I see evidence of this . . . how will it inform my instruction?	If I see evidence of this . . . how will it inform my instruction?	If I see evidence of this . . . how will it inform my instruction?	

TOOL 11

RUBRIC QUALITY REVIEW WORKSHEET

Assessment/Task:

Date: Reviewer(s):

Questions for Evaluating Rubric Quality	Comments/Feedback for Each Review Question
1. Do the number of performance levels and rubric format make sense? ☐ Format matches purpose and use ☐ Adjacent performance levels are qualitatively different ☐ Levels reflect how completion of the task might naturally progress with instruction	
2. Is descriptive language maximized? ☐ Little or no judgmental language (e.g., rough, poor, messy, impressive) used. ☐ Avoids vague/subjective language (e.g., ample, mostly) and frequency indicators (e.g., often, frequently, rarely).	
3. Do descriptors emphasize quality over quantity (relevant descriptive details v. three details)? Or a descriptive use of numbers describes parts completed (e.g., I can complete part one of the research).	
4. Do descriptors state performance in the positive—what IS happening, rather than what is NOT happening? ☐ Lowest levels focus on beginning stages ☐ Describes a (planned) progression of learning ☐ Have student work samples or piloting informed performance descriptions? ☐ Every performance level describes what students CAN do.	
5. Do descriptors describe excellent *rather than* perfect performance? ☐ Describes a progression from Novice to Expert performance ☐ Performance descriptors increase with depth, complexity, and/or breadth of knowledge ☐ Minor errors not weighted more than quality of ideas or thinking	
6. Do rubric language and criteria match rigor expectations of task? ☐ A range of criteria align with task expectations (form, accuracy, process, impact, construction of knowledge) ☐ Not limited to basic skills and concepts or routine tasks ☐ At least one criterion builds to transfer and construction of knowledge or deeper understanding	
7. Is the language kid friendly? ☐ Could this be used for peer- and self-assessment? ☐ Have students had input into the writing or refinement of performance level descriptions?	

ADDITIONAL NOTES

TOOL 12

STUDENT WORK ANALYSIS

Analyzing and Acting on Evidence

Subject Area: **Grade Level:**

Unit/Topic: **Performance Task:**

How used? ☐ **Pre/formative** ☐ **Mid/Interim** ☐ **Post/Summative**

Date administered:

Content Standards Assessed:

Intended Depth-of-Knowledge (DOK) Level(s): ☐ DOK 1 ☐ DOK 2 ☐ DOK 3 ☐ DOK 4

☐ 1. **Using district or classroom assessment or rubric, describe expectations for performance.**
(See wording of prompt, standards-specific rubric, Hess CRM, and/or standards to determine desired expectations.)

☐ 2. Quickly "sort" students' work by degree of objectives met. List student name or % in each category so you can track progress over time with each major assessment. (a) **Start by sorting two larger piles: met or not met.** You may also need a "not sure" pile at this point. (b) **Re-sort each pile**: not met = partially met but close vs. minimal; met = met vs. met plus more. (c) **Distribute any remaining work samples** by matching them to typical work from each set.

This is not scoring!

Objectives not met	Objectives partially met	Objectives fully met	Objectives fully met and exceeded
% of class	% of class	% of class	% of class

(*continued*)

TOOL 12

STUDENT WORK ANALYSIS

Analyzing and Acting on Evidence

Subject Area: **Grade Level:**

Unit/Topic: **Performance Task:**

How used? ☐ **Pre/formative** ☐ **Mid/Interim** ☐ **Post/Summative**

Date administered:

Content Standards Assessed:

Intended Depth-of-Knowledge (DOK) Level(s): ☐ DOK 1 ☐ DOK 2 ☐ DOK 3 ☐ DOK 4

☐ 1. **Using district or classroom assessment or rubric, describe expectations for performance.**
(See wording of prompt, standards-specific rubric, Hess CRM, and/or standards to determine desired expectations.)

☐ 2. Quickly "sort" students' work by degree of objectives met. List student name or % in each category so you can track progress over time with each major assessment. (a) **Start by sorting two larger piles: met or not met.** You may also need a "not sure" pile at this point. (b) **Re-sort each pile**: not met = partially met but close vs. minimal; met = met vs. met plus more. (c) **Distribute any remaining work samples** by matching them to typical work from each set.

This is not scoring!

Objectives not met	Objectives partially met	Objectives fully met	Objectives fully met and exceeded
____ % of class	____ % of class	____ % of class	____ % of class

TOOL 13

RIGOR BY DESIGN

LESSON AND UNIT PLANNING TEMPLATE

Unit or Project : Grade Level:

Essential or Driving Question (Big Idea):

DOK Levels	Teacher Roles	Planned Strategies Observable Evidence	Student Roles	Observable Evidence of Learning
1 **Acquire Foundation**	☐ Questions to focus attention (*Who? What? Where? How? When?*) ☐ Directs, leads, demonstrates, defines ☐ Monitors practice ☐ Scaffolds for access and focus		☐ Acquires vocabulary, facts, rules, routines ☐ Memorizes, recites, quotes, restates ☐ Retrieves information, uses required tools and resources ☐ Practices and self-monitors routine skills ☐ Seeks support, asks questions to clarify procedures or task expectations	
2 **Use, Connect, Conceptualize**	☐ Questions to build schema: differentiate parts from whole, classify, explain relationships (*Can you explain examples/ non-examples? Cause-effect?*) ☐ Draws out basic inferences ☐ Models/scaffolds conceptual understanding (*Why? Under what conditions?*) ☐ Provides guided practice for multi-step tasks		☐ Explains relationships, sorts, classifies, compares, organizes information, summarizes ☐ Makes predictions based on estimates, observations, prior knowledge ☐ Proposes problems, topics, or questions to investigate ☐ Raises conceptual questions (*Why? What if?*) ☐ Selects tool or strategy for specific purpose ☐ Follows teacher-designed procedures	
3 **Deepen & Construct Meaning**	☐ Questions to probe reasoning, thinking, planning (*How will you know or do this? Where is the evidence?*) ☐ Promotes peer discourse & self-reflection to uncover Big Ideas, themes ☐ Designs tasks requiring proof, justification, analysis of evidence quality and accuracy ☐ Models/scaffolds validating sources ☐ Supports student-designed performance tasks		☐ Uncovers relevant, accurate, credible information, flaws in a design, or proposed solutions linked with Big Ideas, themes ☐ Raises questions that explore underlying meanings (*Is this what the author is saying? What can we learn from this?*) ☐ Plans how to develop supporting (hard) evidence for conclusions, solutions, or claims ☐ Researches, tests and revises ideas, solves non-routine problems ☐ Sets goals, monitors progress ☐ Self-assesses; uses feedback to improve quality	
4 **Extend, Transfer, Broaden Meaning**	☐ Questions to challenge or to extend meaning (Big Ideas, themes), explore sources, broaden perspectives (*Are there potential biases? Can you propose an alternative model?*) ☐ Models/scaffolds triangulating sources, peer-to-peer critique, self-reflection ☐ Supports student-designed performance tasks ☐ Promotes peer discourse & self-reflection to uncover Big Ideas, themes		☐ Initiates, transfers, and *constructs* new knowledge, insights linked to Big Ideas, themes ☐ Modifies, creates, elaborates based on analysis and interpretation of multiple sources ☐ Raises novel questions and investigates real-world problems and issues ☐ Sets goals, monitors progress ☐ Self-manages time ☐ Generates self-reflections; self-asesses and uses feedback to improve quality	

Observation Note Catcher

LESSON OBSERVATION FORM FOR VIDEO CLIPS OR LESSON OBSERVATIONS

PART 1: Work with a partner to watch a video clip of a lesson. One person observes/notes teacher actions; the other observes/notes student actions. Describe the task students are doing. Capture *specific words* of teacher and student questions and comments.

My Notes: What the teacher did	My Notes: What students did

PART 2: Compare observations. Discuss what the teacher might do next to deepen the learning.

Teacher Look-Fors	Student Look-Fors
• Asks probing questions at different DOK levels to build schema, uncover reasoning, engage *all* • Strategically scaffolds to support access to complex content or to support completion of complex tasks • Designs instruction that moves from foundational (taking in) to conceptual (connecting) to deeper understanding (construct knowledge) • Designs discourse questions or complex tasks that press for explanations, require evidence to support reasoning • Asks questions to challenge or extend thinking • Invites student input into task design (content, processes, or products) • Supports metacognition (during learning) and reflection (before or after learning) • Frames feedback specific to student questions, responses, rubric criteria, or student work products • Promotes collaboration/discourse to spark substantive student inquiry, or to uncover Big Ideas or themes	• Engage in discourse about concepts, relationships (cause–effect; compare-contrast), observations, predictions (if/then) • Raise conceptual questions • Generate questions or pose problems to investigate • Self-manage group work/collaboration, task completion • Uncover relevant, accurate, credible information • Uncover flaws in a design, plan, or proposed solution • Develop and use supporting evidence for conclusions, solutions, claims, or point of view • Research, test, and refine ideas, solutions, claims • Solve nonroutine problems • Self-assess using feedback to improve quality or deepen understanding • Initiate, transfer, and construct new knowledge linked to Big Ideas or themes • Investigate real-world problems and issues • Create/modify/elaborate on ideas based on analysis of information from multiple sources • Set goals, monitor progress

References

Ainsworth, L. (2024). *Integrating teaching and learning: "Timeless" essentials for creating integrated units of study* (Vol. 1). BookBaby.

Almarode, J., Fisher, D., Thunder, K., & Frey (2021). *The success criteria playbook: A hands-on guide to making learning visible and measureable*. Corwin.

Anderson, L., Krathwohl, D., Airasian, P., Cruikshank, K., Mayer, R., Pintrich, P., Raths, J., & Wittrock, M. (Eds.). (2001). *A taxonomy for learning, teaching, and assessing: A revision of Bloom's taxonomy of educational objectives*. Addison Wesley Longman.

Andrade, H. (2016). *Arts assessment of and for learning*. NYC Department of Education. http://artsassessmentforlearning.org/about-assessment/

Armstrong, P. (2017). *Bloom's taxonomy*. https://cft.vanderbilt.edu/guides-sub-pages/blooms-taxonomy/

Arundel. K. (2024, May 13). Rapid guessing on tests increases after lunch, study finds. *K-12 Dive*. https://www.k12dive.com/news/assessments-testing-disengagement-lunch/715886/

Banner, I. (2016). *Teachers' perspectives and development of academic rigor: An action research study* (Doctoral dissertation, University of Bridgeport). https://www.academia.edu/73274274/Teachers_Perspectives_and_Development_of_Academic_Rigor_An Action_Research_Study

Becker, A. (2013a). *Journey*. Candlewick Press.

Becker, A. (2013b). *Quest*. Candlewick Press.

Berger, R., Woodfin, L., & Vilen, A. (2016). *Learning that lasts: Challenging, engaging, and empowering students with deeper instruction*. John Wiley and Sons.

Biggs, J., & Collis, K. (1982). *Evaluating the quality of learning: The SOLO taxonomy (structure of the observed learning outcome)*. Academic Press.

Biggs, J., & Collis, K. (1989). Towards a model of school-based curriculum development and assessment using the SOLO taxonomy. *Australian Journal of Education, 33*(2), 151–163.

Blackburn, B. R. (2023). *Rigor in your classroom* (2nd ed.). Routledge.

Bloom, B. S. (Ed.) (1956). *The taxonomy of educational objectives, the classification of educational goals, handbook 1: Cognitive domain*. David McKay Company.

Bloom, B. S. (1968). Learning for mastery. *Evaluation Comment* (UCLA-CSIEP), *1*(2), 1–12.

Boaler, J. (2019). *Why struggle is essential for the brain—and our lives*. EdSurge. https://www.edsurge.com/news/2019-10-28-why-struggle-is-essential-for-the-brain-and-our-lives

Brown, C., & Mednick, A. (2012). *Quality performance assessment: A guide for schools and districts*. Center for Collaborative Education.

Brown, P., Roediger, H., & McDaniel, M. (2014). *Make it stick: The science of successful learning*. Belknap Press of Harvard University Press.

Center for Depth and Complexity. (n.d.). *About the depth and complexity framework*. https://depthcomplexity.com/about-depth-complexity

Chiappetta, E. (April, 2023). *A collaborative approach to mistake analysis*. Edutopia. https://www.edutopia.org/article/collaborative-approach-mistake-analysis

Clark, B. (1983). *Growing up gifted* (2nd ed). Charles E. Merrill Publishing Company.

Common Core State Standards Initiative (CCSSO). (2010a). *Common core state standards for English language arts and literacy in history/social studies, science, and technical subjects*. CCSSO and National Governors Association.

Common Core State Standards Initiative. (2010b). *Common core state standards for Mathematics/CCSSM*. Council of Chief State School Officers and National Governors' Association.

Costley, J., & Fanguy, M. (2021). Collaborative note-taking affects cognitive load: The interplay of completeness and interaction. *Educational Technology Research and Development, 69*, 655–671. https://doi.org/10.1007/s11423-021-09979-2

Cree, V. & McCauley, C. (2000). *Transfer of learning in professional and vocational education*. Psychology Press.

de Bono, E. (1999) *Six thinking hats: An essential approach to business management*. Little, Brown and Company.

Dixon, C. (n.d). *Much ado about teaching: Elevating discussion with TQE.* https://muchadoaboutteaching.com/elevating-discussion-with-tqe

Doyle, S., Lieberman, S., & McDonald, L. (2006). *The transfer of learning: Participants' perspectives of adult education and training.* Gower Publishing, Ltd.

Fisher, D., Frey, N., Amador, O., & Assof, J. (2020). *The teacher clarity playbook: A hands-on guide to creating learning intentions and success criteria for organized, effective instruction.* Corwin.

Fisher, D., Frey, N., & Hattie, J. (2016). *Visible learning for literacy: Implementing the practices that work best to accelerate student learning.* Corwin.

Fitzhugh, G. (2019). *A comparison of complex thinking required by the elementary New Jersey student learning standards and past New Jersey curriculum standards* [Doctoral dissertation, Seton Hall University]. https://scholarship.shu.edu/dissertations/2613/

Gardner, H. (2006). *Multiple intelligences: New horizons* (Rev. ed.). Basic Books.

Gonser, S. (September, 2021). *Ron Berger on the power of 'beautiful work.'* Edutopia. www.edutopia.org/article/ron-berger-power-beautiful-work

Guerrero, T., Griffin, T., & Wiley, J. (2023). *The effects of generating examples on comprehension and meta comprehension.* ResearchGate. https://www.researchgate.net/publication/373687803_The_effects_of_generating_examples_on_comprehension_and_metacomprehension

Harte, C., & Barrett, T. (2021). *5 ways to power-up your teaching with the SOLO taxonomy [Video file].* YouTube. https://www.youtube.com/watch?v=nStNc0ZCkH4&t=3s

Hattie, J. (2009). *Visible learning: A synthesis of over 800 meta-analyses relating to achievement.* Routledge.

Hattie, J. (2023). *Visible learning: The sequel—A synthesis of over 2,100 meta-analyses relating to achievement.* Routledge.

Hattie, J., & Brown, G. (2004, September). Cognitive processes in asTTle: The SOLO taxonomy. asTTle Technical Report #43, University of Auckland/Ministry of Education. https://www.scribd.com/document/393641190/43-The-SOLO-taxonomy-2004-pdf

Heldsinger, S. (May, 2021). *Teacher moderation that contributes to effective teaching.* https://www.brightpath.com.au/articles/teacher-moderation-that-contributes-to-effective-teaching

Hess, K. (2005). *Exploring cognitive demand in instruction and assessment.* ResearchGate. https://www.researchgate.net/publication/237469037_Exploring_Cognitive_Demand_in_Instruction_and_Assessment

Hess. K. (2009). *The Hess cognitive rigor matrices (CRMs).* Educational Research in Action. www.karin-hess.com/cognitive-rigor-and-dok

Hess, K. (2013). *Linking research with practice: A local assessment toolkit to guide school leaders.* Educational Research in Action.

Hess, K. (2018). *A local assessment toolkit to promote deeper learning: Transforming research into practice.* Corwin.

Hess, K. (2021). *The rigor by design playbook: The what, the why, and the how.* Educational Research in Action.

Hess, K. (2023). *Rigor by design, not chance: Deeper thinking through actionable instruction and assessment.* ASCD.

Hess, K., Carlock, D., Jones, B., & Walkup, J. (2009). *What exactly do "fewer, clearer, and higher standards" really look like in the classroom? Using a cognitive rigor matrix to analyze curriculum, plan lessons, and implement assessments.* https://www.karin-hess.com/_files/ugd/5e86bd_2f72d4acd00a4494b0677adecafd119f.pdf

Hess, K., Colby, R., & Joseph, D. (2020). *Deeper competency-based learning: Making equitable student-centered, sustainable shifts.* Corwin.

Hess, K., & Gong, B. (2014). *Ready for college? Achieving the Common Core standards and beyond through deeper, student-centered learning.* https://www.karin-hess.com/_files/ugd/5e86bd_56a017e0741a4141b3d27676240dab3a.pdf

Hess, K., & Kearns, J. (2010). *Learning progressions frameworks designed for use with the* Common Core state standards in mathematics K-12. National Alternate Assessment Center at the University of Kentucky and the National Center for the Improvement of Educational Assessment. http://www.karin-hess.com/learning-progressions

Hess, K., & Kearns, J. (2011). *Learning progressions frameworks designed for use with the* Common Core state standards for ELA & literacy, K-12. National Alternate Assessment Center at the University of Kentucky and the National Center for the Improvement of Educational Assessment. http://www.karin-hess.com/learning-progressions

Hess, K., McDivitt, P., & Fincher, M. (2008). *Who are the 2% students and how do we design test items and assessments that provide greater access for them? Results from a pilot study with Georgia students.* https://www.researchgate.net/publication/365838020_Who-are_the_2_students_and_how_do_we_design_test_items_and_assessments_that_provide_access

Hess, K., Stack, B., & Vander Els, J. (2025). *Elevating competency-based learning in a PLC at work: Actionable assessment, defensible evidence, and equitable grading.* Solution Tree Press.

Hewlett Foundation. (2013). *Deeper learning competencies.* https://hewlett.org/wp-content/uploads/2016/08/Deeper_Learning_Defined_April_2013.pdf

Hilger, L. (July 2023). *What's the difference between a standard and a competency?* KnowledgeWorks. https://knowledgeworks.org/resources/difference-between-standard-competency

Hougen, M. C., & Smartt, S. M. (2020). *Fundamentals of literacy instruction & assessment* (2nd ed.). Paul H. Brookes Publishing.

Howard, G. (1991, November). Sally Forth comic strip. King Features Syndicate, Inc.

Jacobs, H., & Zmuda, A. (2023a). *Streamlining the curriculum: using the storyboard approach to frame compelling learning journeys*. ASCD

Jacobs, H., & Zmuda, A. (February, 2023b). Storyboarding your curriculum. *Educational Leadership, 80*(5). ASCD. https://www.ascd.org/el/articles/storyboarding-your-curriculum

Kagan, S. (1992). *Cooperative learning*. Resources for Teachers.

Levine, E., & Patrick, S. (2019). *What is competency-based education? An updated definition*. Aurora Institute. https://aurora-institute.org/resource/what-is-competency-based-education-an-updated-definition

Luther, M. (,2024, April 5). *Using collaborative slide decks to promote engagement*. Edutopia. https://www.edutopia.org/article/using-slide-decks-collaborative-learning

McTighe, J., & Silver, H. (2020). *Teaching for deeper learning: Tools to engage students in meaning making*. ASCD.

National Academies Press. (2001). *Knowing what students know: The science and design of educational assessment*. Author.

National Academies Press. (2012). *Education for work and Life*.

National Association for Sport and Physical Education. (2004). *National standards for physical education* (2nd ed.).

National Research Council. (1999). *How people learn: Brain, mind, experience, and school*. National Academies Press.

National Research Council. (2000). *How people learn: Brain, mind, experience, and school: Expanded edition*. National Academies Press. https://doi.org/10.17226/9853

Nelson, D., & Zayed, J. (2019). *Cognitive rigor: Augmenting writing skills in the EFL classroom. Journal of Education and Practice, 10*(9). 83–94.

Nottingham, J., Nottingham, J., & Renton, M. (2017). *Challenging learning through dialogue: Strategies to engage your students and develop their language of learning*. Corwin.

Oakley, B., Rogowsky, B., & Sejnowski, T. (2021). *Uncommon sense teaching: Practical insights in brain science to help students learn*. TarcherPerigee.

Owens, K. (June, 2024). *Sketchnotes help kids grow their mindsets*. MiddleWeb. https://www.middleweb.com/46197/sketchnotes-help-kids-grow-their-mindsets

Perkins, D., & Salomon, G. (1988) Teaching for transfer. *Educational Leadership, 46*(1), 22–32.

Porter, A., & Smithson, J. (2001). Defining, developing, and using curriculum indicators (CPRE Research Report Series RR-048). Consortium for Policy Research in Education.

Sackstein, S. (2024). *Student-led assessment: Promoting agency and achievement through portfolios and conferences*. ASCD.

Schwartz, K. (May, 2016). *Why the language we use about learning determines inclusivity*. MindShift. http://ww2.kqed.org/mindshift/2016/05/18/why-the-language-we-use-about-learning-determines-inclusivity

Society of Health and Physical Education. (2024). New national physical education standards. Shape America. http://shapeamerica.org

Sousa, D. (1995). *How the brain learns*. National Association of Secondary School Principals.

Sousa, D. (2015). *Brain friendly assessments: What they are and how to use them*. Learning Sciences International.

Sousa, D. (2022). *How the brain learns* (6th ed.). Corwin.

Spencer, J. (March, 2024). Making time for project-based learning (PBL). Blog post. https://www.spencerauthor.com/pbl-time

Sriram, R. (2020, April 13). *The neuroscience behind productive struggle*. Edutopia.https://www.edutopia.org/article/neuroscience-behind-productive-struggle

VanderArk, T. (2017). *How schools develop student agency*. Aurora Institute. https://www.competencyworks.org/insights-into-implementation/how-schools-develop-student-agency

Vygotsky, L. S. (1978). *Mind and society: The development of higher mental processes*. Harvard University Press.

Webb, N. (1997). Research Monograph Number 6: Criteria for alignment of expectations and assessments on mathematics and science education. CCSSO.

Webb, N. (2002). *Depth-of-knowledge levels for four content areas*. https://www.maine.gov/doe/sites/maine.gov.doe/files/inline-files/dok.pdf

Webb, N. (2005). *Web alignment tool (WAT): Training manual*. University of Wisconsin and Council of Chief State School Officers. https://watv2.wceruw.org

Webb, N., Christopherson, S., & Morelan, B. (March, 2023). *An inside look at Webb's depth of knowledge*. Edutopia. https://www.edutopia.org/article/how-use-norman-webb-depth-of-knowledge

Wiggins, G. (2006). *Healthier testing made easy: The idea of authentic assessment*. Edutopia. www.edutopia.org/authentic-assessment-grant-wiggins

Wiggins, G. (2012). *Transfer as the point of education*. Authentic Education. https://authenticeducation.org/transfer-as-the-point-of-education/

Wiggins, G., & McTighe, J. (2005). *Understanding by design*. ASCD.

Wiggins, G., & McTighe, J. (2011). *The understanding by design guide to creating high-quality units*. ASCD.

Wiliam, D., Fisher, D., & Frey, N. (2024). *Student assessment: Better evidence, better decisions, better learning*. Corwin.

Willingham, D. (2017). *The reading mind: A cognitive approach to understanding how the mind reads*. Jossey-Bass.

Index

The letter *t* or *f* following a page number refers to a table or figure, respectively.

About the Author

Karin Hess, author of the Hess Cognitive Rigor Matrices, is recognized internationally as a leader in developing practical approaches for using depth of knowledge, cognitive rigor, and learning progressions as the foundation for formative, interim, and performance-based assessment. Her 26 years working in schools include 15 years as a classroom teacher, and as an elementary and middle school principal and district curriculum director.

For almost 15 years at the Center for Assessment in Dover, New Hampshire, Karin distinguished herself as a curriculum and assessment expert in multiple content areas. She has effectively guided over 40 U.S. states and territories in the development of grade-level expectations and test specifications for both general education and alternate assessments for significantly cognitively disabled students. She has authored and coauthored more than a dozen books or book chapters, and numerous articles and white papers related to DOK/cognitive rigor applied to instructional practices, alignment, and assessment. Karin's books applying DOK include *A Local Assessment Toolkit to Promote Deeper Learning* (Hess, 2018); *Ready to Advance PreK Curriculum* (Gibson, Cárdenas-Hagan, & Hess, 2019); chapters in *Assessing Students in the Margins* (Russell & Kavanaugh, 2011) and *Fundamentals of Literacy Instruction and Assessment, Prek-6, Second Edition* (Hougen & Smartt, 2020); *Deeper Competency-Based-Learning* (Hess, Colby, & Joseph, 2020); *Rigor by Design, Not Chance* (Hess, 2023), and *Elevating Competency-Based Learning in a PLC at Work: Actionable Assessment, Defensible Evidence, and Equitable Grading* (Hess, Stack, & Vander Els, 2025).

Karin has worked as the New Jersey state director of gifted education, program evaluator for the Vermont Mathematics Project, as co-developer and editor of *Science Exemplars* for six years, and content specialist for development of many state assessment blueprints, including the New England Common Assessments in ELA, math, and science (NECAP) and the Smarter Balanced Assessment Consortium (SBAC) content specifications for the *Common Core State Standards* in ELA and mathematics. Her varied projects enable her to understand the practical implications of her work while maintaining fidelity to research, technical quality, and established best practices. Over the years, she has also been a technical adviser to EL Education in establishing criteria for high-quality student work; Mentoring Minds; Achieve3000; the Quality Performance Assessment Project (Brown & Mednick, 2012) and the New Hampshire Learning Initiative in guiding the design of performance-based assessments and rubrics; the New Meridian (assessment) Corporation, India's EKSAQ reading assessments, Renaissance Learning, and World-Class Instructional Design and Assessment (WIDA) in applying cognitive rigor and learning progressions research to their work.

Karin currently works to guide and support school districts and states in implementing competency-based learning systems and creating and analyzing the use of high-quality interim and performance-based assessments.

You can follow Karin on LinkedIn or bluesky social @Drkarinhess or on her website at https://www.karin-hess.com/blog-1.